What people are saying abc

Ron Harris' writing is consistent with h
years of delightful "iron sharpens iron" friendship. His style is punchy but light on
foot, challenging always, yet often with a welcome, underlying humour. In this excellent book, we are faced with a series of remarkable insights—sometimes gentle
and sometimes startling. It is this consistent "spirit" insight that I find most appealing, demanding a pause for reflection after each chapter. Through this book I have
been enriched and also sometimes a little shaken in the latent areas of my thinking.
I commend it to everyone who is hungry for the truth.

—Jeff Steady, Pastor
Malvern Hills Life Church
New Frontiers (ret.) & Transform Work, U.K.

Ron and myself have been good friends and involved in various Christian ministries
for more than forty-five years. I am very pleased he has taken the time to write *Not
Dressed for the Occasion*—it is a gift to the church. He is a gifted leader and outstand-
ing communicator. Over the past few years, he has written many short articles that
many find instructional and inspiring. I have found his articles to be very applicable
to my daily life. As a result, I am more sensitive to the Holy Spirit's leading, have a
better understanding of the secrets of the Kingdom, and experience improved in-
terpersonal relationships with others. I am sure you will find this book a very easy
read—easy to understand and very useful in small group meetings for discussion. I
highly recommend it.

—Rev. Brian Devitt, Pastoral Counsellor
The Embassy Church
Oshawa, Ontario, Canada

It is an honour to commend to you this book written by my friend, Ron Harris. I
can attest to the honesty and wisdom this work embodies. His desire to see people
grow in a maturity that embraces both knowledge and practical applications of the
Father's love is evident in the words of this book. Having known Ron and his wonderful wife, Brenda, has made my life, as well as the lives of many others, richer. He
is "a man after God's own heart."

—Dan Chappell, Prophetic and Teaching Ministry
The Fellowship Christian Church
US and Canada

RON
HARRIS
WITH
CHRISTINE
WINTER

NOT
DRESSED
FOR
THE
OCCASION

NOT DRESSED FOR THE OCCASION
Copyright © 2018 by Ron Harris with Christine Winter

Cover photograph by Oliver Steins.

All rights reserved. Neither this publication nor any part of this publication may be reproduced or transmitted in any form or by any means, electronic or mechanical, including photocopying, recording or any information storage and retrieval system, without permission in writing from the author.

The views and opinions expressed in this publication belong solely to the author and do not reflect those of Word Alive Press or any of its employees.

Unless otherwise indicated, scripture quotations are taken from the New American Standard Bible®, Copyright © 1960, 1962, 1963, 1968, 1971, 1972, 1973, 1975, 1977, 1995 by The Lockman Foundation. Used by permission. Scripture quotations marked (NIV) are taken from the Holy Bible, NEW INTERNATIONAL VERSION®, NIV® Copyright © 1973, 1978, 1984, 2011 by Biblica, Inc.® Used by permission. All rights reserved worldwide. Scripture quotations marked (KJV) are taken from the Holy Bible, King James Version, which is in the public domain. Scripture quotations marked (TLB) are taken from The Living Bible copyright © 1971 by Tyndale House Foundation. Used by permission of Tyndale House Publishers Inc., Carol Stream, Illinois 60188. All rights reserved. The Living Bible, TLB, and the The Living Bible logo are registered trademarks of Tyndale House Publishers. Scripture quotations marked (PHILLIPS) are taken from The New Testament in Modern English by J.B Phillips copyright © 1960, 1972 J. B. Phillips. Administered by The Archbishops' Council of the Church of England. Used by Permission. Scripture quotations marked (NKJV) are taken from the New King James Version®. Copyright © 1982 by Thomas Nelson, Inc. Used by permission. All rights reserved. Scripture quotations marked (NLT) are taken from the Holy Bible, New Living Translation, copyright ©1996, 2004, 2007 by Tyndale House Foundation. Used by permission of Tyndale House Publishers, Inc., Carol Stream, Illinois 60188. All rights reserved. Scripture quotations marked (OMNB) are taken from The One New Man Bible, copyright © 2011 William J. Morford. Used by permission of True Potential Publishing, Inc. Scripture quotations marked (MSG) are taken from The Message. Copyright © by Eugene H. Peterson 1993, 1994, 1995, 1996, 2000, 2001, 2002. Used by permission of NavPress Publishing Group.

Printed in Canada

ISBN: 978-1-4866-1676-3

Word Alive Press
119 De Baets Street, Winnipeg, MB R2J 3R9
www.wordalivepress.ca

Cataloguing in Publication may be obtained through Library and Archives Canada

CONTENT

INTRODUCTION

Several years ago, I was motivated to write articles from a Christian world viewpoint for a local newspaper. In the last three years, that activity has been directed to our local congregation and now perhaps a much larger audience through this book. I believe there is place for the Christian view to be applied to our personal life experiences, our behaviour, the local church, and world situations. *Not Dressed for the Occasion* touches on politics, history, sexuality, social agendas, and theology. Nothing is sacrosanct from the debate.

This book is an accumulation of experiences and my attempt at capturing them in short articles with the hope that they can be of value to others. They are the result of my walk with God, my professional career, involvement with all levels of leadership in local churches, and, not least of all, my opportunity to experience many cultures in the business world around the globe. I have been an itinerant business traveller for many years, and this has enabled me to see something of the real differences that each nation and culture has developed and how they impact my Christian world view.

Originally I had no intention of turning these articles into a book, but I experienced something of a revelation from God that simultaneously scared and elated me. As I reread some of the articles, I had the most unusual experience of feeling that they were not mine—they were someone else's work. Christine Winter has been my right hand in advising, editing, and suggesting changes, but that was not what I encountered; it was not "our work." Because I have gone through this process a thousand times in the creative world of interior design, I knew that this was totally different.

As I mused, I recalled that I had experienced this before when teaching or preaching. I was moving in another dimension than my natural man. I was speaking beyond myself. My religious mind screamed, "Heresy! He thinks he is God," so I checked my heart for the arch enemy, pride. I know him well; he is no stranger to me, but I saw nothing. At this point I appealed to God in prayer to help me understand what was happening, and this is what I heard. You be the judge: *"For we are his workmanship, created in Christ Jesus for good works, which God has prepared beforehand so that we would walk in them"* (Ephesians 2:10). Was this a manifestation of his workmanship? *"But we all, with unveiled face, beholding as in a mirror the glory of the Lord, are being transformed into the same image from glory to glory, just as from the Lord ... the Spirit"* (2 Corinthians 3:18). Perhaps part of the transforming from glory to glory? Then I thought of the ultimate intention for us all: *"until we all attain to the unity of the faith, and to the knowledge of the Son of God, to a mature man, to the measure of the stature which belongs to the fullness of Christ"* (Ephesians 4:13). I leave you to meditate on that one!

To further endorse my experience, I was reminded of a series of meetings I led in the U.K. where, after preaching, I would then pray for everyone who indicated the desire. One time out of the corner of my eye I noticed a youngish couple following me as I moved from person to person. Eventually I stopped, turned to them, and asked "Can I pray for you both?"

I was stunned by the reply of, "No, it's like watching Jesus." I was totally oblivious of myself; my complete focus was to bless those I was praying for, and at that moment I had become in their eyes Jesus. Heresy? It is a common saying that the only Christ this world will see is us, His church, and we will not even be aware of those moments. My desire is that it would be 24/7 for me.

My hope is that those who read this book will garner some knowledge and understanding of life, but most of all be transformed into the image of His Son. In that sense, my appeal is primarily to Christians of any age who are open to learning from my life, but it's also for those who have never embraced the Christian faith. It's my prayer that this book will be a window into my world view and thinking. I write from the perspective of someone who has been a follower of Christ for over six decades.

Shalom.

1.
FEEL YOU DON'T COUNT?

MANY TIMES I AM IMPACTED BY THE EVENTS HAPPENING TO OUR FAMILIES AND churches both locally and internationally. They all appear bigger than me, and I feel controlled by them, as though I were a pawn in their game. Some people get to achieve great power or influence and they use it to control churches, homes, and nations, but my observations reveal that this very controlling ends up destroying both the controller and the controlled. We are witnessing this destruction in countries around the world; however, there is resistance. I've also seen that, as Christians, we have weapons for the "mass blessing" of people and for the annihilation of principalities and powers ruling over those churches, homes, and nations. This opportunity to bring "mass blessing" is our responsibility as Christ's church, but how do we do this in the light of such opposition?

The answer is *prayer*—not the feeble "bless me Lord" variety, but the taking of the sword of the Spirit and praying with both understanding and in the Spirit. Seeing ourselves as God's representatives of His Kingdom on earth is the most effective weapon the church can exercise. Prayer is the most powerful weapon on earth for defeating the enemy and delivering God's people. The fact that we pray so little and that our prayers are focused mostly on our own well-being means we have not been effective in impacting history for Christ.

We need to learn how to pray as David prayed; Lord, teach us to pray! "... *teacheth my hands to war*"[1] not against people, but against those spiritual forces in high places.

"*The Lord hath prepared his throne in the heavens; and his kingdom ruleth over all.*"[2] From the natural, carnal man's standpoint, this appears foolish. But from God's position, He has called us to be co-workers with Him through the process of prayer: "*your kingdom come, your will be done ...*"[3] The weapons of our warfare are mighty through God to the pulling down of strongholds.

---

1   Psalm 18:34 (KJV).

2   Psalm 103:19 (KJV).

3   Matthew 6:10 (NIV).

We have relied on the wisdom of man. We organize and plan seminars, conferences, and programs, but God asks us to take the sword of prayer out of the sheath, clean it off, and do battle for His Kingdom in the heavens as well as on earth.

God's power can only be released through prayer. We cannot change ourselves, but as we pray, He changes us and the circumstance around us. God has His part and we have ours. In God's view, everything is provided, but we must take the sword of the Spirit and pray. We need Holy Spirit-anointed prayer. He has delegated authority and power to His church, but we stand impotent! Because we have been so ineffective, the enemy of our souls has ravaged us, our homes, our churches, our bodies, and our nations. You say, "But isn't God sovereign?" "*The earth is the Lord's, and the fullness thereof; the world, and they that dwell therein.*"[4]

God *gave* the land of Canaan to the Israelites, but it was full of wicked, cruel, demon- worshipping tribes. What sort of gift is this? How would we in this modern age like those sorts of gifts for Christmas, when we get frustrated because the kids complain that it's too difficult to rip off the plastic wrapping?

The process of possessing the land, God's gift, was twofold: Firstly, He owns the original design. It was and is God's by creative right, despite the fact that it was polluted by sin and Satan. Secondly, it was necessary to develop God-like character in His people so that they could rule the land in righteousness. "*... the battle is the Lord's,*"[5] but we must take it by His power and authority with the same purpose in mind—taking possession of the land from an already-defeated enemy who pretends he still owns it. Though futile, the adversary continues defending every last inch, using lies and deceit and hoping we will believe them.

"*And there we saw the giants, the sons of Anak ...*"[6] but "*... the one who is in you is greater than the one who is in the world.*"[7] We need to heed the word God gave to Joshua: "*Every place that the sole of your foot shall tread upon, that have I given unto you, as I said unto Moses.*"[8] Our part is to set our foot, and it is always on someone else's—the enemy's! Take no prisoners, because they will do the same as the existing inhabitants in Canaan—they will infect us with their sin.

We cannot be passive if we are to possess the land. Jesus said: "*... the kingdom of heaven suffereth violence, and the violent take it by force.*"[9] Remember that our

---

4   Psalm 24:1 (KJV).

5   1 Samuel 17:47 (NIV).

6   Numbers 13:33 (KJV).

7   1 John 4:4 (NIV).

8   Joshua 1:3 (KJV).

9   Matthew 11:12 (KJV).

weapons are God's provision and they are spiritual, not natural. Man's planned programs, seminars, brilliant teaching and preaching, and even conferences will not cut it. They are helps, but it is the troops on the ground, God's infantry, that is needed—that's you and me persevering in anointed Holy Spirit prayer.

God is looking for an army—not of conscripts, but of those who volunteer "to suffer with Him," to fight to the death of the enemy by the sacrifice of their own lives. This is the time; this is the season; this is the call to take God's most powerful weapon of "mass blessing" and pray until we see the Kingdom of God rise in power in the earth.

"*Thy kingdom come, thy will be done* ... [10] (emphasis added).

The church militant! "... *the sword of the Lord, and of Gideon*"[11] (emphasis added).

Shalom.

---

10   Matthew 6:10 (KJV).

11   Judges 7:18 (KJV).

2.
MADE IN HIS IMAGE AND LIKENESS—BEAUTY

ONE OF THE CHARACTERISTICS OF MAN'S NATURE IS HIS ABILITY TO APPRECIATE beauty. If we approach this experience with the view of the "evolutionist," this encounter with beauty has no rational explanation for existence. For most people, the "theory of evolution" has become the "fact of evolution," so one must ask, "Where in that process did this intangible pleasure 'evolve?'"

I have observed agnostics and atheists waxing eloquent about the awesome beauty of this species of animal or insect, a cosmic happening, or a scenic view of earth. But what is the source of such ability to enjoy an insight into the material universe, or even the simple pleasure of viewing a mountain or stream? Those who discard the idea of creation say, "Surely they are only the result of the folding earth's crust and the moving tectonic plates." Why the pleasure experience?

We seem to be able to find beauty in almost any aspect of life, from the simplest life forms observed under a microscope to the complexity of man's brain, the uniqueness of snowflakes, or the majesty of the Rocky Mountains. These pleasurable experiences of beauty become entrenched memories that we keep in order to savour them at a later date, but we also look for opportunities to share them with others. The very act of sharing brings a new dimension to this encounter with beauty that is not only different but often deeper and richer than the original experience. It is as though the original engagement is not complete until we have found others with whom to share it. Those who find no pleasure in beauty are thought to need some form of therapy, or as lacking some important human quality of life.

The biggest question then is not "Why are things beautiful?" but "Why do we find them beautiful and then need to share this experience with others?"

One of the confirmations of God's existence is that we repeat His process of creation; we create watches, cars, and buildings—none of which evolve but are deliberate decisions and acts by mankind. Creation is a God procedure, and because we are made in His image and likeness, we repeat the Creator's process. We just can't stop creating!

Beauty is such a vital part of this creative process that even the success of automobile sales rises and falls on their visual beauty. This illustration can be extended to all walks of life. Technology has to be clad in beauty for us enjoy it more fully. Ugly houses people do not buy.

But is "beauty only in the eye of the beholder"? Well, to some degree, yes, but there is a process of increasing human capacity to embrace higher degrees of every subject. The joy of music follows the same parallel; we start with simple melodies and progress to more and more complex sounds. So it is with beauty; it is conditioned and developed by both experience and exposure. Even so, this still does not explain the sense of wonder and awe we encounter when exposed to something totally new to our sight: "*The heavens declare the glory of God; the skies proclaim the work of his hands. Day after day they pour forth speech; night after night they reveal knowledge.*"[12]

The higher value we place on an object, the greater the level of pleasure. For example, our pleasure encountering insects will be less than with cats, dogs, and horses. The reason for this progression is that we enjoy feedback and response to our enjoyment of these creatures. A relationship is developed between the parties involved. This leads us to human relationships, where we find that beauty is often the door of attraction between men and women. There is a very profitable industry built on this intangible experience of creating, improving, and maintaining beauty.

We can now see how beauty is linked to the potential of relationships, but there is another dimension of beauty that the eye does not see—that of the beautiful qualities of life, the fruit of God's Holy Spirit, which is love, joy, peace, patience, kindness, goodness, faithfulness, gentleness, and self control.[13] These "God qualities" point us to at least two conclusions: First, man is designed to delight in people, objects, values, character, and other qualities, as well as desire to share these pleasures and experiences with others. This is what the Bible calls worship. The second is that this encounter also changes us. The degree of change will depend on our reaction to that in which we delight. We embrace the splendour we see in beautiful things and acquire them so that we can extend the enjoyment. In terms of people, we plan to share time with them or even marry them. The more time and effort we invest in these encounters, the more we are changed by them and become like them. Sometimes the dog owner starts to look like the dog!

The ultimate transformation occurs when we see the beauty of God's character of mercy, love, and forgiveness balanced with justice and righteousness. The degree of exposure to such beautiful qualities has the impact of us desiring to be like Him.

For this we were made, created in his image and likeness. But you say, "Mankind is a nothing like this. The world is not a pretty picture. How can this be?" Well, that is

---

12   Psalm 19:1–2 (NIV).

13   Galatians 5:22.

the reason for Jesus Christ's teaching, His life, and humiliating murder on a Roman scaffold. Human nature has an ugly side. It indulges in filth and cruel behaviour and is completely opposite to our ability to embrace beauty. The vandal in us wants to spoil all that is beautiful. We break windows, bully, kill, steal, hurt, and destroy all that is wholesome and beautiful. Some go as far as to describe these activities as being beautiful, but in reality, we know they are only perversions.

The appeal of Christianity as expressed in Christ is the process of dealing with both the cause of our failure and our restoration to the ultimate vision—made to be like God. Don't you think this is something so important that it's worth exploring further?

Shalom.

3.
CORPORATE MIND—UNITY IN DIVERSITY

ONE OF THE UNIQUE EXPRESSIONS OF GOD'S CREATION IS THE "CORPORATE mind." You may well ask, "What is the corporate mind and what has this to do with our Christian life and walk?" If you place heart cells from different people in a Petri dish in a laboratory setting, all of them will beat with the beat of their own original heart. But soon, as if an unseen hand is guiding them, a miracle takes place and gradually all hearts beat with the same rhythm. This same miracle applies to five million flying starlings that are able to make incredibly fast course changes as though they were one bird.

What is the unseen hand that makes them move as one? In a similar, miraculous way schools of small fish confuse their large predators by flowing in the same way as the birds. Where is the conductor of these brilliant manoeuvres? Huge herds of animals migrate across the African plains as though driven by herdsmen, but with no leader or organization. Millions of monarch butterflies travel thousands of miles as though hearing the call of some distant destiny. What is the unseen hand that makes them move as one? Human beings rage in mobs of violence, striking terror and destruction in their path as though guided by one angry hand. Who drives this ride of death?

One hundred and twenty souls waited in an upper room for a promise of an encounter with God that would change the world, in "…one accord in one place."[14] They experienced a divine encounter enabling them to fulfill the great commission of Christ to make disciples of all nations.

In the natural kingdom, scientists are at a loss to explain this ability of multiple numbers of creatures acting as one mind, but for Christ's body, the church, God gives us the key. The "one accord and one place" orchestrated by the Holy Spirit is the uniting of God's sovereign timing of Pentecost and the unity of men.

A reporter from the London Daily newspaper visited the Welsh Revival in 1904 and wrote of his experience, noting that the recognized leader, Evan Roberts, appeared not to be leading. "The last person to control the meeting in any way is Evan Roberts. You feel that the thousand or fifteen hundred persons before you have

---

14   Acts 2:1 (KJV).

become merged into one myriad-headed but single soul personality ... Repentance, open confession, intercessory prayer, and above all this marvellous musical liturgy—a liturgy unwritten, but heartfelt mighty chorus like the thunder of the surge on the rock-bound shore ... And all this vast quivering, throbbing, singing, praying, exultant multitude intensely conscious of the all-pervading influence of some invisible reality ... They call it ***the Spirit of God***"[15] (emphasis added). We recognize, and to varying degrees experience, this corporate mind when we flow together as we "sing and pray in the Spirit."

The first expression of this "oneness" is the revelation of God (Elohim) as being triune: Father, Son, and Holy Spirit. Jesus prayed for His disciples "... *that they may be one as we are one—I in them and you in me—so that they may be brought to complete unity. Then the world will know that you sent me* ..."[16] I believe the world has yet to see that prayer fulfilled—the church moving as one, the body of Christ by the Holy Spirit, "*your kingdom come, your will be done, on earth as it is in heaven.*"[17] Now.

Paul urged the church in Ephesus: "*Be completely humble and gentle; be patient, bearing with one another in love. Make every effort to keep the unity of the Spirit through the bond of peace. There is one body and one Spirit* ..."[18]

I am praying, working, seeking, knocking, thirsty, hungry, and desperate so that I may do my part to be in one accord, in one place, for the sovereign timing of God, to have my heart cells beat with heart cells of others who beat with God's heartbeat and all who have His heart for each other and the lost.

"... *that they may be one as we are one* ..."[19]

Shalom.

---

15   Rick Joyner, *World Aflame* (Charlotte, NC: Morning Star Publications, 1993), 71.

16   John 17:22–23 (NIV).

17   Matthew 6:10 (NIV).

18   Ephesians 4:2–4a (NIV).

19   John 17:22 (NIV).

4.
CORPORATE WORSHIP—
SOME THOUGHTS

OVER THE LAST FORTY YEARS, THE INTENT OF CORPORATE WORSHIP OF GOD HAS been restored to one similar to the worship exercised during King David's reign. The roots of this restoration can be traced to several sources—Afro-American Christians, the Jesus People revival, the Charismatic movement, and in Toronto, Canada, with a strong Jewish flavour, the "Catacombs" youth movement led by Merv and Merla Watson. This form of worship was birthed by Christians "baptized in the Holy Spirit," and they had both expectations and experiences of the Holy Spirit's gifts and ministry. Today, most evangelical churches enjoy various expressions of this type of worship, but for those of us who were at its inception, our focus is seeing it developed as the work of Christ with our relationship to God the Father as the prime theme.

Some feel that the requirement to collectively worship in the usual standing position is not how they would like to express their devotion; their preference is to read scripture or just sit silently during the twenty to sixty-minute time frame. But is this action a valid expression of corporate worship? The psalms are replete with encouragements to shout, sing, dance, raise hands, and use every form of musical instrument: *"Be glad in the Lord, and rejoice … and shout for joy, all ye that are upright in heart"*[20] This directive is also found in the entirety of Psalm 150. We are not short of biblical encouragement for this collective activity of worshipping God.

The issue lies in the choice between the "I" prefer and the "we" together. Even though the actions themselves are "spiritual" and appear not to conflict with the collective activity of worship, in reality sitting silently with head down and habitually reading scripture does contradict the community direction. For example, the "I" and the "we" become obvious if I decide to sing out loud during a time of teaching because I prefer it to collective listening. The impact on the corporate, however, is the same in terms of unity of action, unity of purpose, and unity of focus on God.

Is there then room for expression of the gifts of the Spirit and/or scripture revelation? Well, yes … it's outlined by Paul in 1 Corinthians 14 as being *led by the spirit*. The point is, habitually doing something different than sharing in an activity requiring collective expression produces actions that are under the control of "self,"

---

not the "body." If my right hand consistently refuses to work when my body needs it (and has the ability to do so), then the solution of Jesus is rather severe—cut it off, because it is in rebellion.

OBJECTIONS:

1. "Now," you may say, "I can't sing, never have, and never will." Well, the Psalms encourage us to make a joyful noise and shout to the Lord.[21] If you can't carry a melody, then speak the words out loud with those who sing.

2. "I don't think the words are scriptural, and when I read the Bible, I am reading the real Word of God." This appears to be very spiritual, but if you cannot find any songs with which you agree with all the words, then you have an even bigger problem. May God show you the root, because it could endanger your soul.

3. Using the same rationale, you may say, "I can justify not listening to the one speaking or teaching on the basis that they are not as 'scriptural' as reading the Bible, so I will read while they speak." The "I" is not engaging collectively. There is no gift of "being an arm chair critic to evaluate every word sung or spoken." We are members of a living body, and that requires continual, corporate involvement.

4. "I always worship in silence." Try that one on your spouse when he or she asks you a question or for some feedback. You cannot do this habitually in any arena of life, other than a monastic order devoted to a vow of silence. You will find no support in scripture for "habitual silence," just punishment for failing to believe God's Word through an angel!

5. Now for the less than spiritual excuses: "I must answer this text message;" "I need to carry on with this conversation;" "My hair needs the final-touch up;" "I wonder if so and so is coming today."

"*There is a right time for everything … a time to be quiet; a time to speak up.*"[22]

"*Enter into his gates with thanksgiving, and into his courts with praise: be thankful unto him, and bless his name.*"[23]

"*Let everything that hath breath praise the Lord.*"[24]

You are excluded from this command only if you do not have breath! I recommend reading this in conjunction with the article "Corporate Mind" to see the full potential of worship.

Shalom.

---

21   Psalm 100:1.

22   Ecclesiastes 3:1, 7b (TLB).

23   Psalm 100:4 (KJV).

24   Psalm 150:6 (KJV).

5.
NON-CONSUMING FIRE

I STARED INTO THE FLAMES OF A FIRE I HAD LIT TO CLEAR UP A PILE OF SMALL branches from three fir trees that my grandson had pruned last year. Cottage country permits open fires two hours after sunrise and two hours before sunset. I was transfixed by the capacity of the flames to consume both the dry and wet wood that I had thrown into its hungry mouth. Even though we used an old truck wheel rim to keep the fire from spreading, some of the twigs from the branches fell outside of it. Steam rose from the limbs of the wet branches that at first seemed to resist the power of the flames, but they too soon joined their brothers in the dance of fire. A once living thing was soon to become nothing but ash.

The falling ash started to cover branches not yet totally consumed, and it consequently prevented the lifeblood of oxygen from reaching all its members. In order to allow air into the centre of the fire, I used a larger branch to lift the remaining limbs. Immediately flames burst out of the middle of the dry cedar branch, but when I withdrew it from the fire, it soon lost its ability to burn. All that remained was a blackened stub. For the fire to continue its chain reaction, it needed to be fed a new combustible material and a continuous supply of oxygen. Once removed, branches quickly ceased to burn; fire is a corporate experience.

Moses had a similar experience in the desert as he watched in amazement how the bush was burning but not consumed to ash. Out of this fire came the voice of God's angel, calling him to be the messenger of deliverance to the children of Israel from four hundred years of Egyptian slavery.

The 120 followers of Jesus were obedient to His last instruction before His ascension, and they waited in prayer ten days for the promise of the Holy Spirit. They had no previous experience to guide their expectations, nor did they have any knowledge of what the promise would be or how it would be fulfilled.

Luke explains:

And when the day of Pentecost was fully come, they were all with one accord in one place. And suddenly there came a sound from heaven as of a rushing mighty wind, and it filled all the house where they were sitting. And there appeared unto them cloven tongues like as of fire, and it sat upon each of them.

And they were all filled with the Holy Spirit and began to speak with other tongues, as the Spirit gave them utterance.[25]

As I sat in a recent prayer meeting, I saw a vision of flames rising into the night sky. I couldn't see the source of the fire, but the dancing flames sent glowing ashes into the heavenly realm. I was aware that the flames from our prayer group illuminated the night sky and were a sign of our worship rising to God. My understanding was that our worship was penetrating "the heavenlies" way beyond our small group.

As I continued to meditate on the vision, out of this fire came the word, "Tonight I am starting a fire that cannot be put out. It will become a wildfire that has no limits." We were in the "one accord and one place" of God's purposes. We were to be the bush that Moses experienced. We were to be the bush fed by the oxygen of the Holy Spirit, burning but not being consumed.

In the cottage fire experience, I saw that it is not a one-person event. In order to enable a chain reaction of God's power and purpose, it is necessary for the fire to be a collective, corporate encounter. Branches taken out of the fire soon die.

Fire needs an "ignition point," someone or something to start the process. In the context of the destruction of all that is unholy, the writer to the Hebrews states: "… *God is a consuming fire,*"[26] but that same fire also brings light to a world under the darkness of the night sky.

The word came to me: "Will you throw your branch onto God's fire so that it spreads to all around you? Man cannot control this fire, and it has no limits. It will be a wildfire, and the wind of the Spirit will allow it to leap across the nations."

"*And all the world will see that I, the Lord, have set the fire. It shall not be put out.*"[27]

Shalom.

---

25   Acts 2:1–4 (KJV).

26   Hebrews 12:29 (NIV).

27   Ezekiel 20:48 (TLB).

6.
CHRISTIAN EXTREMIST FUNDAMENTALIST GROUP

CHALLENGED BY A COMMITMENT TO FOLLOW THE TEACHING AND BEHAVIOUR of their founder, Jesus, a group of extremist fundamentalist Christians are invading parts of Canada and announcing their plans for a new state they call "the Kingdom of God." It has been reported that these radical fundamentalists have infiltrated and recruited followers from a variety of Christian denominations in order to further their cause. A few of the ministers and priests from these denominations have spoken out against these extremists and expressed their surprise when they discovered some of these fundamentalist "cell groups" in their own churches.

These terrorists have no fear of death and are prepared to give up everything, including their lives, for this *Kingdom of God*. These radicals, who are attempting to convert everyone to belief in Jesus (the prophet, priest, and king of this new kingdom), have issued a nation-wide warning that there is no safe place to hide. The "violence" perpetrated by some of these fundamentalists is unprecedented as they engage in acts such as feeding the poor, helping the broken-hearted, speaking encouraging words to the downhearted, praying for those in authority, healing the sick, doing miracles of blessing, working for justice for all, and sharing the good news of the *Kingdom of God*.

Reports have verified that these radicals willingly commit "suicide" by dying to their own lives for the sake of others. This seems to confirm the previous report that there is no safe place to hide from their extreme acts of forgiveness, mercy, and kindness. These extremists prey on the downtrodden of society by introducing them to the power of Almighty God in the name of their founder, Jesus, who in turn delivers and heals drug addicts, alcoholics, broken relationships, and marriages.

There are also reports confirming that these extreme fundamentalists consider the materialism of the capitalist societies to be a false god, and they preach that "souls" are more important than possessions. It seems evident that nothing can stop their nation-wide plan to invade churches, mosques, schools, universities, businesses, and even homes with their "violent" and extremist messages of "convert and receive forgiveness, mercy, and hope."

Do you recognize any of these Christian fundamentalist extremists?

A final thought: After reading the last paragraph of this article, I was struck by the similarity of the Islamic and Christian directive to convert the entire world to their respective faiths. Though the eternal destination and method of conversion of Islam and Christianity are completely opposite, Islam's edict—convert or die—is true for both. Selah.

Shalom.

7.
A TALE OF TWO KINGDOMS

I WAS RECENTLY PRAYING AND REHEARSING THE "LORD'S PRAYER" WHEN I CAME to the phrase "your kingdom come, your will be done, on earth as it is in heaven."[28] I was struck by the fact that a Sovereign God has asked us to pray and be part of bringing this to pass. This led me to observe that I could freely choose or reject to partner with God to achieve His plans.

As Christians, we understand that there are only two kingdoms—the Kingdom of God and the kingdom of Satan. (Jesus teaches this clearly in John's Gospel.) I suddenly realized that one of the major differences between the two was freedom versus control, and we see this expressed through two world religions. Biblical Christianity invites, pleads, and calls people to repent and accept Christ as Lord and Saviour. Islam's Koran, on the other hand, states that you either convert or die— freedom versus control.

I recall the Discipleship Movement of the 1980s. Although it contained many good disciplines, it was rooted in control. Elders controlled the saints, including simple decisions like whether or not they could buy a fridge. Though not always successful, through the generations, Christianity has fought control, even from its birth in the book of Acts. Being British, I recall the history of the Reformation and how the progression of control led to division within in the church at large. The controlling Church of Rome encouraged the Spanish Catholics to invade England, then one hundred years later these same Reformers imprisoned the Baptists, forbidding them to meet for worship—control versus freedom. Though the divide and conquer strategy is highly effective, controllers will use any means to exterminate freedom.

Remember, there are only two kingdoms, and it's been my observation that a pattern exists. When Christianity, regardless of denomination, turns to controlling the saints, it becomes Satan's kingdom, not God's. Control is the vehicle Satan uses in order to provoke rebellion against God. In the wilderness, he even tried to control Jesus by offering Him "the kingdoms of this world and their splendor"[29] if He would only fall down and worship him. It's this same principle at work when pastors

---

28   Matthew 6:10 (NIV).

29   Matthew 4:8 (NIV).

control churches, boards control pastors, Christians control one another, a husband controls a wife, or the reverse. It applies to empires and dictatorial rulers controlling millions—it's not just North Korea. Muslim countries have such difficulty functioning as democracies because there is no freedom in Islam, only bondage. Slavery is rooted in Satan's kingdom and manifests itself by one person exercising total control over another for life and death.

The Apostle Paul appeals to the church in Galatia; *"You foolish Galatians! Who has bewitched you?"*[30] *"It is for freedom that Christ has set us free. Stand firm, then, and do not let yourselves be burdened again by a yoke of slavery."*[31] Religion brings slavery through the law; Christ brings freedom through grace.

The picture now hits even closer to home when Paul tells the Christians in Rome that whatever controls us makes us its slave. Every habit, addiction, and sin that controls us makes us behave like those in the "other kingdom," but the good news is that Jesus came to set us *free* from the law of sin and death. But how are we to understand Paul's letter to the church in Philippi when he says *"that at the name of Jesus every knee should bow, in heaven and on earth and under the earth, and every tongue acknowledge that Jesus Christ is Lord, to the glory of God the Father"*?[32] Isn't that control? There's a story of a child who when standing in his high chair is told to sit down but then states, "I will sit down, but I am still standing up in my heart." All will bow the knee and confess that Jesus is Lord, but as to their hearts, only God knows.

When Jesus was accused of performing healings and miracles by the power of Satan, He replied, *"Any kingdom divided against itself will be ruined, and a house divided against itself will fall."*[33] Satan's kingdom is united in its plan to control mankind, but it's God's kingdom plan to set us free. That's demonstrated in Luke's Gospel in the story of Jesus healing a crippled woman who had been bent over for eighteen years: "whom Satan has kept bound."[34]

So now my prayer is Your kingdom come in me first, then this church, then this region, then this province then this nation, even unto the ends of the earth. Your will be done in me first, then this church, then this … just like it is in Heaven.

God has given us freedom to impact history for His Kingdom by prayer. In whatever colour it paints itself, let us not allow the "other kingdom" to control us.

Shalom.

---

30   Galatians 3:1a (NIV).
31   Galatians 5:1 (NIV).
32   Philippians 2:10–11(NIV).
33   Luke 11:17b (NIV).
34   Luke 13:16 (NIV).

8.
TRENCH WARFARE

ONE OF THE DESCRIPTIONS OF THE FIRST WORLD WAR FROM 1914 TO 1918 WAS that it was a "battle of the trenches," but being in the trenches had never been the plan. It was to be mobile and fast, but instead it became bogged down in a stationary, bloody war of attrition. Masses of men and material were thrown into battle, achieving a mere few yards of enemy territory only to be faced with equally devastating counterattacks from an enemy trying to hold their position.

Christians are also participants in a war, but unlike the earthly battle, ours is a "war in the heavenlies." Life is not all prosperity and blessing, because we face an adversary who is determined to spoil all the good. In his letter to the Ephesians, Paul outlines not only the structure of enemy forces but also God's provision of battle gear of armour and weapons. He tells us that we must stand to the end, regardless of what or when that end is. This is the Christian version of the "stand your ground" legislation adopted by some states in the US.

The more determined we are to see the Kingdom of God established in our lives and churches, the more determined the enemy is in counter-attacking our initiative. This is a "war in the trenches," and every inch of ground we take for God we face opposition from our adversary.

Some of us have been taking part in the "move of God" weekly prayer meeting with a view to achieve our goal of seeing more of the Kingdom of God ruling in both our lives and our church. There have been various results; some have made great gains, others smaller, but all seem to have moved out from their trenches to engage and defeat the enemy.

The challenge now is to retain the victories and the ground we have taken. Some have experienced serious counterattacks as Satan tries to repossess his control. We know that we have been assured of our ultimate victory, but that does not deter our foe. Every success we achieve in God will be tested and challenged by the accuser.

The question I now ask myself is, "Have I allowed my passion to see the Kingdom of God come more fully in my life and the church to falter or grow cold?" We had a prophetic word in our last "move of God "prayer meeting where God encouraged us not to be discouraged but to persevere, for He is with us.

Shalom.

9.
PARASITE OR PARACLETE

BRENDA AND I WATCHED A DAVID SUZUKI *NATURE OF THINGS* TV SHOW ON THE topic of parasites. We were amazed by the brilliance of these creatures as they first invaded then controlled their hosts. These parasites feed on and reproduce in their hosts, and while most have no brains, some can still migrate through four different subjects in order to reproduce their species. By invading the brain of the host, these parasites are capable of manipulating and controlling behaviour for their own benefit, even though they have no brains of their own.

How can something with no brain or obvious source of intelligence carry out such amazing feats to obtain control? What or who is the source? I thought of Paul's illustration regarding the parasite of the sin-nature:

> *My own behaviour baffles me. For I find myself not doing what I really want to do but doing what I really loathe. Yet surely if I do these things that I really don't want to do ... it cannot be said that "I" am doing them at all—it must be sin that has made its home in my nature ... I often find that I have the will to do good, but not the power.*[35]

Just as a parasite cannot exist without a host, so sin cannot reproduce its nature without a human being; "... *each* [reproducing] *according to its kind.*"[36] Satan takes advantage of this parasite of sin and will claim us for his kingdom if we let him. He and his demons become the parasites that can either control and possess our lives or oppress us, but our enemy's objective is always to control us. The ultimate battleground is the mind; if he can control our thoughts, he can steer the vessel.

As the Apostle Paul states: "*Who will free me from my slavery to this deadly lower nature? Thank God! It has been done by Jesus Christ our Lord. He has set me free.*"[37] Without going into all the details of this wonderful plan of deliverance, He provides a *Paraclete* to take up residence in us.

---

35   Romans 7:15b–20 (PHILLIPS).

36   Genesis 1:24 (NIV).

37   Romans 7:24–25 (TLB).

Paraclete is a transliteration of a Greek word meaning the "Holy Spirit." When we turn our lives over to God, accepting Jesus as Saviour and Lord, this blessed Paraclete makes His home in our spirit, and as Paul states: "*Don't let the world around you [or the parasite of sin] squeeze you into its own mould, but let God re-mould your minds from within, so that you may prove in practice that the plan of God for you is good ...*"[38] Or as another translation puts it "*... but be transformed by the renewing of your mind.*"[39]

The salvation process works the same as the parasite, but the methods and results are totally different. The parasite comes in uninvited and steals control of your mind for its own ends, but the Paraclete comes only by invitation, responding only to our willingness to cooperate and submit our will to His. Our behaviour is no longer controlled by the parasite of sin but led by the powerful Holy Spirit of God ... if we let Him.

The Paraclete's ultimate goal is to mould the character and behaviour of Jesus Christ in us; only then can we become one with each other and with God: "*that they all may be one, as You, Father, are in Me, and I in You; that they also may be one in Us, that the world may believe that You sent Me.*"[40]

Come, Holy Spirit, come; come, Holy Spirit, come; come, Holy Spirit, come ... Shalom.

---

38   Romans 12:2 (PHILLIPS).

39   Romans 12:2 (NIV).

40   John 17:21 (NKJV).

10.
VISITATION OR HABITATION

WHILE READING GRAHAM COOKE'S BOOK, *A DIVINE CONFRONTATION*, I WAS struck by the phrase "visitation or habitation."[41] Since we had already studied Rick Joyner's book *World Aflame* (a history of the ten-month Welsh Revival in 1904), I focused on God's intent with that revival, as well as the ones that followed. I couldn't help wondering why all these resurgences seemed to have such a short shelf life. Were these manifestations just "visitations" of God, or was the Divine intent something more permanent, a "habitation"?

Two years after the Welsh Revival there was little evidence of its existence—pubs were full, crime increased, chapels and prayer meetings were empty. Why was there so little apparent fruit remaining? There was fruit, but it wasn't obvious if you looked only at what remained on the tree. Much of what was produced during the revival had fallen to the ground, but Jesus said, *"Very truly I tell you, unless a kernel of wheat falls to the ground and dies, it remains only a single seed. But if it dies, it produces many seeds."*[42] Even though a lot of the fruit fell to the ground, some of it did die and produced several of the Pentecostal movements in the U.K. Both the Assemblies of God and the Elim Church were founded by two brothers (Stephen and George Jeffries) who were saved in that revival. The Apostolic Church also has its roots in the same experience with the restoration of the five-fold ministries of apostle, prophet, evangelist, pastor, and teacher.

While studying the revival, we examined its strengths and reviewed its weaknesses, and though we can glean a lot from studying strengths, we can sometimes learn even more from weaknesses. The principle figure, Evan Roberts, was subject to physical burnout, which sadly led to his spiritual seduction. It appears that Jessie Penn Lewis managed to control Evan by suggesting that he was taking too much of the glory. That was the last thing Evan wanted. Tragically, he believed the charge and withdrew from the revival. Some years later, he co-authored a book with Jessie Penn Lewis particularly condemning manifestations and speaking in tongues.

---

41   Graham Cooke, *A Divine Confrontation* (Shippensburg, PA: Destiny Image, 2000), 53–54.

42   John 12:24 (NIV).

The Welsh Revival became only a visitation of God's presence, not a habitation. Jacob's experience at Bethel was no different—both were only visitations: "*This is none other than the house of God, and this is the gate of heaven.*"[43] There's only problem with that—God is not in the hotel business. He is a "home maker." If we won't go to Him, He will come to us: "*... they shall call his name Emmanuel, which being interpreted is, God with us.*"[44] Jesus came and lived with us for thirty-three years. He drank water and wine; He ate bread and meat. His visit was a habitation, not a visitation. God is here to stay!

Jesus promised that, "*My Father's house has many rooms; if it were no so, I would have told you ...*"[45] There are "many rooms in heaven," a place of eternal habitation, but what about now? Solomon states, "*I have built You a lofty house, and a place for Your dwelling forever.*"[46] Paul reveals that Christians are "*... being built together to become a dwelling in which God lives by his Spirit.*"[47] The climax of the ages in Revelation is that, "*God's dwelling place is now among the people, and he will dwell with them.*"[48]

The promise now is that God will dwell in us both individually and corporately: "*... Christ in you ...*"[49] and "*... the body of Christ ...*"[50] "*And you now have become living building-stones for God's use in building his house.*"[51]

With the manifest presence of God comes the glory of God. His glory was so immensely displayed at the completion of the tabernacle and temple that the priests were unable to minister. At Pentecost, the manifestation of God's presence was more personal; He is, "*Emmanuel, which being interpreted, is God with us.*"[52]

My prayer is to see us live, inhabit, and dwell in the manifest presence of God in our individual and congregational lives habitually. Let us turn every visitation into a habitation for God's presence ... that's His will and purpose, to dwell (tabernacle) with man.

More to come ...

Shalom.

---

43   Genesis 28:17.
44   Matthew 1:23 (KJV).
45   John 14:2a (NIV).
46   2 Chronicles 6:2.
47   Ephesians 2:22 (NIV).
48   Revelation 21:3 (NIV).
49   Colossians 1:27 (NIV).
50   1 Corinthians 12:27 (NIV).
51   1 Peter 2:5a (TLB).
52   Matthew 1:23 (KJV).

11.
BREAKDOWN, BREAKTHROUGH, AND BREAKOUT

LIFE AND THE HUMAN CONDITION ARE NEVER STATIC; THEY ARE ALWAYS MOVING, but the question is, "In which direction are they going?" For more than two and a half years I have been on a personal pilgrimage in pursuit of the manifest presence of God in both my personal life and that of the church. The reason for my pursuit is that the Word of God (scriptures) indicates that the prime reason for God creating man was "... *for thy pleasure they are and were created.*"[53] To delight and please God includes our sharing His pleasure in His presence.

The purpose for the atoning work of Jesus was to enable us to engage in His presence, but there are many hindrances preventing the breakthrough of that enjoyment. God has, in Christ, removed all the roadblocks and walls preventing us from enjoying fellowship with Him. When Jesus cried from His cross, "*It is finished!*"[54] the curtain of the Holy of Holies in the temple was ripped from top to bottom. Our breakthrough involves entering the breakthrough Jesus has achieved for us.

This is where the issue of breakdown or breakthrough is created. They seem at first to be opposites, but they are complementary. The biggest hindrance to God's manifest presence is me. Self stands at the door of my heart, and the only way to break through is to allow God to break down that door; the only condition is that He is will only do it with my cooperation. If I fill my house with myself, there is no room for God. What we often interpret as the tribulations of life are in fact God's process of bringing us to a place of "breakdown of self" so that we can enter the "breakthrough of His presence." This breakthrough and breakdown experience is a process; oh, how I wish it was a one stop deal! "... *Except a corn of wheat falls into the ground and die, it abideth alone: but if it die, it bringeth forth much fruit.*"[55]

For all who dare to come on this pilgrimage, there is a personal and corporate breakdown and breakthrough being experienced. One of the areas generating this process is the realm of private and corporate prayer; there is an ongoing release of prayer both in the Spirit and with understanding. Our call is to engage in Holy Spirit

---

53   Revelation 4:11b (KJV).

54   John 19:30b (KJV).

55   John 12:24–25 (KJV).

prayer encounters so that we stay tender toward the Spirit Himself. Without this continual divine encounter our hearts become like the skin that develops over paint in an open can—they quickly harden. Like Jesus, our hearts must become as innocent as a child, free from all pride and open to hearing the Father's voice: "*I tell you the truth, the Son can do nothing by himself. He does only what he sees the Father doing.*"[56]

Our pursuit of His heart to delight and please Him is producing the breakthrough worship that we are experiencing each week, and in the process, we are being changed "*... from glory to glory, even as by the Spirit of the Lord.*"[57]

What then is the purpose of breakthrough? It is that we might engage in God's manifest presence and bring delight to His heart. We will then become a dwelling place, a habitation for God among us. When God comes in His manifest presence, He breaks out into our families, our community, our region, and to the uttermost parts of the world, and it is from this position that we impart God's heart of salvation for all.

Pentecost becomes our pattern. Empowered by His Spirit, we break out from our buildings into the community with the true-heart of God. The challenge for us is that we need to experience *breakdown* before we achieve *breakthrough* in order to enable *breakout*.

Shalom.

---

56   John 5:19 (NLT).

57   2 Corinthians 3:18b (KJV).

12.
ONE THING

OUR LIVES ARE INCREASINGLY BEING DRIVEN BY TECHNOLOGY, AND THIS article is an example of one expression, or blessing, of the Internet. The lure of technology is potent and has caused a growing concern among many that the children and youth of today are suffering from "technology addiction." But it isn't just the younger generations who are in danger of addiction. Many of us have become so controlled by various forms of media and communication that we're driven by doing instead of being. We rarely stop to smell the roses. Some of us with the DNA of a "type A" personality are potential candidates and are probably more susceptible to this drive of "always doing" than other personality types. I confess that I have this drive to be continually doing something all the time; rest is viewed as an interruption to activity.

As is my usual pattern, I woke up very early one morning. Recently I'd decided to make notes for a word God had laid on my heart. I was about to reach for my notebook when I heard an almost audible voice saying, "What about Me?" Without a second thought, I realized that because my focus was on doing something for God, in the process I had unintentionally walked right past Him. I stopped, sat, and started repeating the Lord's Prayer as a means of centering my thoughts on my Father; gradually I was able to talk to Him "face to face" as a friend.

As we talked, I discovered that halfway through some statement, God's reply was already there even before I had completed my comments: *"You know what I am going to say before I even say it."*[58] *This is great,* I thought as He shared amazing insights and revelation, but suddenly I noticed that my focus had shifted from Him to the revelation. Once again I reached for my notebook to record what I was seeing. "Stop!" He said. "The Holy Spirit will bring all this to your remembrance. This is *our* time." I have followed His instructions, and although it is a struggle to still the mind, I am reminded of Psalm 46, where in the midst of the battle He shouts, *"**Be still**, and **know** that **I am God**: I will be exalted among the heathen, I will be exalted in the earth"*[59] (emphasis added).

---

58   Psalm 139:4 (TLB).
59   Psalm 46:10 (KJV).

I had drowned out His voice with the subtlest temptation of all—replacing Him with His work. But it doesn't stop there … every good thing can become the enemy of the best, and He is best of all!

David called out to God in his distress; "**One thing** *have I desired of the Lord, that will I seek after; that I may dwell in the house of the Lord all the days of my life, to behold the beauty of the Lord, and to enquire in his temple*"[60] (emphasis added). This is not "work in the house of the Lord," nor is it "teach, preach, sing, or even read scripture … though all of these are good. The most important of all is *dwell*. Jesus said to Martha, "… **one thing is needful**: *and Mary hath chosen that good part …*"[61] (emphasis added).

Shalom.

---

60   Psalm 27:4 (KJV).

61   Luke 10:42 (KJV).

13.
MY AGENDA

We all approach life from our own perspective. Our view of it and its situations are read and influenced through our inherited DNA, family upbringing, local and national culture, religious background (if we have one), and even the climate. This creates in us an expectation mindset that can be called "my agenda," or living my life according to my personal priorities. This might serve our purposes living in isolation, but in the community experience, we're faced with the challenge of blending our agenda with that of others.

Within the denominations of Christianity there are structures and frameworks that either limit our personal agendas completely or allow degrees of freedom of expression of it. God is a relational God and He designed us for community—first with Himself then with others. That's why participating in a community is an important opportunity for us to bond with one another so we can experience the belonging that we all need. The Bible illustrates this involvement as *"the body of Christ,"*[62] with each member being important and valuable.

The challenge is how to structure our relationships in order that each member can function without anyone controlling and dominating. Jesus tells us that *He is the head* and we are the members, and He gave us the Holy Spirit to bond us together in love. The goal is *unity in diversity.* Working it out is the process of learning to submit our personal agendas to God's agenda in conjunction with the rest of "the body." We can only become a functioning part of Christ's body if we die to our own agendas, and the paradox of the reality is that it's only in dying that we find ourselves fully alive and fulfilled. I don't lose myself—I find myself in death to self:

> *Then Jesus said to his disciples, "If anyone wants to follow in my footsteps he must give up all right to himself, take up his cross and follow me. For the man who wants to save his life will lose it; but the man who loses his life for my sake will find it. For what good is it for a man to gain the whole world at the price of his own soul? What could a man offer to buy back his soul once he had lost it?"*[63]

---

62   1 Corinthians 12:27 (NIV)

63   Matthew 16:24–26 (PHILLIPS).

Unless we experience and establish this attitude in our hearts and minds, our personal agendas will cause friction and discord, resulting in a dysfunctional church. Our lives should become expressions of Jesus as our head through the leading of the Holy Spirit, and this can only happen when all individual ambitions are subject to Jesus as the head.

The working out of these principles is found in Paul's instructions:

Accept life with humility and patience, making allowances for each other because you love each other. Make it your aim to be one in the Spirit, and you will inevitably be at peace with one another. You all belong to one body … [64]

Unless we follow this attitude, our personal agendas will be insensitive to the other parts of the body of Christ, and control, manipulation, and domination will rule. It becomes a power-struggle, and we repeat Cain's behaviour by figuratively "murdering" our brother. Cain's violent act was the birth of all war in that all recorded history is marred by blood.

Jesus gave us His peace, but personal and corporate peace is only achieved by dying to our personal agendas, submitting to the lordship of Jesus Christ, and becoming expressions of His life and teaching. This means that in both the structure and interaction of the members of the body of Christ, self must die.

Jesus said that He came to serve, not to be served. Irrespective of our role or office in the church, that is the model for our relationship with each other. He stated that leadership would be identified by a servant's heart. Paul described himself as a *"bond-servant,"* [65] a slave by choice to Jesus and to His body, the church. The motivating power to die to self and become a bond-servant to Christ must be love. Now this may sound too religious and mystical, but Paul explains how the Holy Spirit enables us: "… *the love of God has been poured out within our hearts through the Holy Spirit who was given to us."* [66] My agenda can now become Christ's agenda.

Shalom.

---

64   Ephesians 4:2–4 (PHILLIPS).

65   Romans 1:1

66   Romans 5:5b

14.
JOURNEY INTO THE UNKNOWN

My Vision: I was standing on the shoreline of what I first thought was the sea, but the water became the darkness of the universe in the star-filled night sky. I heard a voice in my spirit saying, "You are standing at the edge of a place of endless, immeasurable revelation of God Himself, and He wants to open up the treasures of Himself to you."

His desire to share Himself with us was both an invitation and an expression of His love. The context was that as Christians we had known and experienced God, but just like the vision of the edges of the sea of the universe, we stopped at the fringes of who He was. It was as though we had drawn an imaginary line as to how far we could go in experiencing and enjoying God this side of heaven. We had stopped at that level of expectation of His calling us into the unknown depths of *Himself*. Yes, Paul said "*... we know in part ...*"[67] but surely this is the call of the Lover for His beloved as described in the Song of Solomon: "*Let him lead me to the banquet hall, and let his banner over me be love.*"[68] It is the cry of Jesus, the bridegroom, for the bride: "*You have stolen my heart, my sister, my bride ...*"[69]

It occurred to me that God's call to Abram to leave his home in Ur and travel to a place unknown carried the promise that we were to be His inheritance: "*... the word of the Lord came to Abram in a vision, saying, Fear not, Abram: I am thy shield, and thy exceeding great reward.*"[70] I understood that to mean that God Himself was *our* great reward and that He manifests the reward by opening up the treasures of Himself to His redeemed creation. As a result, we can enter more fully into an intimate and close relationship with God: "*... Let us make mankind in our image, in our likeness ...*"[71]

Then I recalled Ezekiel's experience of the increasing flow of water from the river under the Temple altar; at first it was only ankle deep, then knee deep, then waist deep, until finally it was so high Ezekiel could not cross. Where the river flowed,

---

67   1 Corinthians 13:9 (NIV).

68   Song of Songs 2:4 (NIV).

69   Song of Songs 4:9a (NIV).

70   Genesis 15:1 (KJV).

71   Genesis 1:26 (NIV).

everything lived. God is inviting us into this river of life (*Himself*) that is so wide, so deep, and so vast that though we can enjoy deep intimacy with Him now, we will never be able to plumb the depths of Him, even throughout eternity.

Will we do as Abram did and respond to His call to journey into the vast unknown of God's love? Are we afraid that we're becoming too heavenly minded to be of any earthly good? Will we be led into a mystical cult experience, or will we find the ultimate goal of existence— God Himself? Abram was encouraged not to fear but to have faith, and that is the call to us today, "*And without faith it is impossible to please God* …"[72] Jesus asked that if we ask for bread, will our earthly fathers give us a serpent. If we ask our heavenly Father for all that is God, will He give us Satan?

Jesus told His disciples that there were things He couldn't tell them because they didn't even understand earthly things. These are some of the things that the natural man cannot conceive or comprehend, but for the hungry, thirsty spiritual man, they are a glorious door of hope. This is the path that opens before us. This is the journey to which He has called us; explore *our* unknown of *Himself*.

"… *you will find him when you search for him with all your heart and soul.*"[73]

Shalom.

---

72   Hebrews 11:6a (NIV).

73   Deuteronomy 4:29b (TLB).

15.
FOR SUCH A TIME AS THIS

"*To every thing there is a season* ..."[74] wrote Solomon as he listed the times of doing and refraining from doing. This experience also applies to the journeys we take as churches, and it is wisdom to know in which season we are and how to respond to it. So in what season are we? As a current-day fellowship of believers, we are in a similar historical setting to that of Queen Esther, in which it could be said that God has brought us together for "... *such a time as this*."[75] We in the Western world may not face extermination as those Christians living under Islamic rule, but God has asked us to die when it is necessary. It was essential for Jesus, so as His followers, it simply goes with the territory.

Wisdom is expressed when we embrace God's call in this specific season. If you recognize this season in both yourself and the church, then this word is not only for you but also for us as a congregation. This church has a history from its inception some thirty-three years ago of looking for a greater revelation and experience of God's manifest presence. They have been years of varied encounters, many of which have been wilderness experiences. However, we have in recent months "... *clean passed over Jordan* ..."[76] and entered "... *the land which he promised* ..."[77] and it's there that we have undergone major personal life changes as well as experienced an increase in God's presence in all our gatherings. Prayer has exploded. The gifts are being manifest, and people are encountering God in new dimensions. These God encounters have resulted in us seeing life more through God's eyes than our own, as well as experiencing an increase of prophetic revelation and praying in the Spirit. There is an expectation of a season that we have never before entertained, the opportunity to explore a new dimension in God. Yet we have an enemy who wants to kill us, but our stand must be as Esther's: "*if I perish, I perish.*"[78] This demands that we lay down all personal ambitions, agendas, and our futures at the feet of our Lord

---

74   Ecclesiastes 3:1 (KJV).

75   Esther 4:14 (NIV).

76   Joshua 4:1 (KJV).

77   Deuteronomy 9:28 (KJV).

78   Esther 4:16 (NIV).

and follow Him: *"... unless a kernel of wheat falls to the ground and dies, it remains only a single seed. But if it dies, it produces many seeds."*[79] We have been warned of some of the challenges we will face—the giants, the armies of the existing inhabitants—but God has trained us in the desert for such a season, for such a time as this.

As "King in waiting," David hid in a cave and gathered around him an assortment of men that were not the "cream of the crop." Similarly, while not wishing to offend anyone, this church is not cut from the finest cloth. We are an assembly of bits and pieces from other families who have made this "cave" our home, but God calls us "David's mighty men of valour" (women too, of course). He has assembled us for "such a time as this" to bring the fullness of God's love, salvation, healing, and deliverance to our world. He has a mandate on His church, and to this one in particular. Remember, God loves stables and He delights in the smallest villages. He is the God of the Nazareths and He has chosen Israel, *"... the fewest of all peoples ..."*[80] for His own. But the enemy has a plan to kill us, and our stand must be as Esther's: "if I perish, I perish."

Who knows if we have come to the Kingdom for such a time as this? If I die, I die. I believe we have come for such a time, and if you share this expectation, then let us strip off everything that hinders us, as well as the sin which dogs our feet. Let us run the race with patience and our eyes fixed on Jesus, who is the source and goal of our faith. If we are to follow and be like Him, then we must do as He did and set our faces like flint for Jerusalem.

"For He Himself endured a cross and thought nothing of its shame because of the joy he had in doing the Father's will."[81]

Shalom.

---

79   John 12:24 (NIV).

80   Deuteronomy 7:7b.

81   J.B. Phillips, *Letters to Young Churches: A Translation of the New Testament Epistles* (London: Geoffrey Bless, 1954), 180.

16.
THE SERVANT GOD—PART 1

THE SERVANT GOD—IS THIS STATEMENT AN OXYMORON, A CONTRADICTION, that God can be sovereign yet the greatest servant of all? God is revealed in Old Covenant Scripture through Israel, and in the New Covenant Scripture through Jesus, Son of Man, Son of God. Paul describes Jesus this way: *"Now Christ is the visible expression of the invisible God ..."*[82]

Most ancient religions see their gods as tyrannical masters of nature and life, demanding human sacrifice at every turn. Even the enlightened Greeks may agree that they were gods made in the image of man, complete with all human weaknesses except with more power. But the Judeo/Christian faiths reveal an understanding of God that shows that we are made in His image: *"So God created mankind in his own image, in the image of God he created them; male and female created he them"*[83] and that God is simultaneously both just and loving.

The New Testament reveals Christ as being *"... the exact representation of his being, sustaining all things by his powerful word."*[84] But does this conflict with the Old Testament portrayal of God? He is described as being so holy that no flesh can look on Him and live: *"... God is a consuming fire"*[85] He is simultaneously depicted as, *"The Lord is merciful and gracious, slow to anger, and plenteous in mercy,"*[86] as well as the One who *"Like as a father pitieth his children, so the Lord pitieth them that fear him. For he knoweth our frame; he remembereth that we are dust."*[87]

On the surface, God seems to be a paradox. He reveals Himself with names that describe His person as, *"The Lord Will Provide,"*[88] *"The Lord Our Righteous*

---

82   Colossians 1:15 (PHILLIPS).

83   Genesis 1:27 (NIV).

84   Hebrews 1:3a (NIV).

85   Hebrews 12:29 (KJV).

86   Psalm 103:8 (KJV).

87   Psalm 103:13-14 (KJV).

88   Genesis 22:14 (NIV).

Savior,[89] *"I am the Lord, who heals you,"*[90] and yet He's the judge of all: *"Will not the judge of all the earth do right?"*[91] These are two sides of understanding His nature and person from the Old Covenant. How can it be that *"God is love,"*[92] yet at the same time be true that God judges all sin? The new Covenant is revealed in Jesus Christ, the expression of God's love and judgement.

The ultimate expression of the Servant God is found in His amazing plan to save mankind from their headlong plunge toward hell. What man could not do to avoid the terrible consequences of his sinful nature and behaviour God bore Himself. Just like a father who so loves his child he dies and sacrifices himself so that the child may live, God has done for all humankind. Scripture defines love this way: *"This is love: not that we loved God, but that he loved us and sent his Son as an atoning sacrifice for our sins"*[93] and, *"Greater love has no one than this: to lay down one's life for one's friends."*[94]

How can this loving God condemn anyone to hell? He states in His Word that *"The Lord is not slow about His promise, as some count slowness, but is patient toward you, not wishing for any to perish but for all to come to repentance."*[95] The key is found in the fact that mankind has been given the gift of free will, giving us the capability of choosing our thoughts and actions. Thoughts lead to actions, and actions have consequences which are either good or bad, and while we are free to make choices, we are not free to choose the consequences of those choices. The only way to avoid the eternal outcome of our sin is to embrace the offer given by the Servant God when He took our place and bore the consequences of our rebellion on Himself in Christ.

God, the ultimate servant, the ultimate lover of mankind, offers the only hope for us, but to reject such love leaves us to personally bear the consequences of our own sin. In this, God is both loving and just. He has done everything He could possibly do to save us.

In Revelation, John states, *"... each person was judged according to what he had done. Then death and Hades were thrown into the lake of fire."*[96] This only happens to

---

89   Jeremiah 23:6 (NIV).

90   Exodus 15:26 (NIV).

91   Genesis 18:25 (NIV).

92   1 John 4:16 (NIV).

93   1 John 4:10 (NIV).

94   John 15:13 (NIV).

95   2 Peter 3:9.

96   Revelation 20:13–14 (NIV).

us if we have chosen to ignore God's solution to save us from the consequences of our own behaviour.

Shalom.

17.
THE SERVANT GOD—PART 2

To us, the greatest demonstration of God's love for us has been his sending his only Son into the world to give us life through him. We see real love, not in the fact that we loved God, but that he loved us and sent his Son to make personal atonement for our sins. If God loved us as much as that, surely we, in our turn, should love each other![97]

LOVE MAKES BOTH PARTIES VULNERABLE. HOMICIDES ARE MORE FREQUENT among "significant others" than any other relationship, so there is always potential for pain. If we reject or fail in our response to His love, does He feel that rejection and pain? In Genesis, God states that because of man's sinfulness, *"The Lord regretted that He had made human beings on the earth, and his heart was deeply troubled."*[98] Isaiah speaks of the Messiah as being *"… despised and rejected by mankind, a man of suffering, and familiar with pain."*[99] Ezekiel states *"I gave you my solemn oath and entered into a covenant with you, declares the Sovereign Lord, and you became mine… But you trusted in your beauty and used your fame to become a prostitute."*[100] You can feel the pain of rejection that God is expressing. In Hosea, His heart is open as He calls, *"I long to redeem them but they speak against me falsely. They do not cry out to me from their hearts but wail on their beds."*[101]

To varying degrees, each of us has experienced the pain of rejection, and we may be able to identify with Jesus when He grieved over Jerusalem; *"… you who kill the prophets and stone those sent to you, how often I have longed to gather your children together, as a hen gathers her chicks under her wings, but you were not willing."*[102]

How I grieve when I hear of child abuse, human trafficking, child slavery, abuse of women (particularly under the control of Islam), and brutal beheadings. I

---

97   1 John 4:9–11 (PHILLIPS).

98   Genesis 6:6 (NIV).

99   Isaiah 53:3 (NIV).

100   Ezekiel 16:8, 15a (NIV).

101   Hosea 7:13b–14a (NIV).

102   Matthew 23:37 (NIV).

experience both pain and anger, and I can only pour out my heart to God in prayer for those so badly treated ... but I am not free of the grief or anger.

What of my complaining about how badly I may have been treated, rejected, insulted, despised, or offended? God for His part knows my thoughts even before I think them, so He continuously experiences this type of detail six and half billion times for each man, woman, and child. His reply to the abused is, "*Like as a father pitieth his children, so the Lord pitieth them that fear him. For he knoweth our frame; he remembereth that we are dust.*"[103] But for the unrepentant who carry out these atrocities, His anger will be revealed. Yes, now I can see how He can be both a God of love and also a God of judgement.

As I drafted this article, I never expected to enter God's pain as intensely as I did when, for a nanosecond, I was allowed to be part of His pain. I recall my vision of being on the seashore, invited by God to enter that "journey into the unknown," and the realization that this experience of seeing the heart of the Servant God was part of the riches of who He is. In light of such love, such mercy, such suffering, all I can do is join the anthem:

> *Then I heard every creature in heaven and on earth and under the earth and on the sea, and all that is in them, saying: "To him who sits on the throne and to the Lamb be praise and honor and glory and power, forever and ever!"*[104]

And I fell down and worshipped ...
Shalom.

---

103 Psalm 103:13–14 (KJV).
104 Revelation 5:13 (NIV).

18.
THE SERVANT GOD—PART 3

THIS WORLD'S SYSTEM IS ALL ABOUT MONEY, POWER, CONTROL, AND domination, but God's Kingdom is just the opposite. It is a clash of two kingdoms, and as Christians we must work only out of God's Kingdom principles. When we choose the methods and motivations of this world's system, we reproduce the fruit of that system, which is death.

Luke records an incident with the disciples in the ministry of Jesus: *"And they began to argue among themselves as to who would have the highest rank in the coming Kingdom."*[105] His response was to explain His attitude about leadership: *"But I am among you as one who serves."*[106] Jesus demonstrated this servant leadership when He humbly took the role of the lowest of slaves and servants by washing the disciples' feet. He told them that *"Greater love has no man than this: to lay down one's life for one's friends,"*[107] and He proved His love by doing that for us all.

Love must be the motive for a true heart to serve. If we serve for any other reason, then we pervert our heart and our actions. Our motives for serving can be good, but as Paul tells us, *"But the greatest of these is love."*[108] We may serve out of obedience but still not love the person we serve. We may serve out of duty, because that is our vocation, but again we can still do it without love. The worst case, however, is serving in order to control, manipulate, or dominate for our selfish benefit.

Because God has revealed Himself as love, all His actions are birthed out of it, even His judgements, discipline, and anger. God becomes angry about man's behaviour toward each other as well as Himself because He cares and loves so much. God does not self-protect, so our behaviour makes Him more vulnerable to suffering. The more you love, the more you can be hurt by those you love. God is no exception, and He feels the pain of it more than we do. If righteous anger rises in us over injustice and cruelty perpetrated by mankind, then how much more in Him?

---

105   Luke 22:24 (TLB).
106   Luke 22:27b (NIV).
107   John 15:13 (NIV).
108   1 Corinthians 13:13b (NIV).

God is more caring than we are, and therefore feels suffering more than we do. He tells us that He is "... *slow to anger, and plenteous in mercy,*"[109] and we're called to be the same. Just as we can cause Him pain through bad behaviour, we can also bring Him pleasure through our loving obedience. Our ability to love comes from Him; "... *because God's love has been poured out into our hearts through the Holy Spirit, who has been given to us.*"[110] Our desire should be to do all we can to please Him, and the expression of that love is serving both God and each other, just as Jesus did.

God wants us to *see* His heart so that we can *know* His heart and *become* His heart so that we become just like His Son. He wants to bring "*many sons unto glory.*"[111] If we have eyes to see, He will show us more intimate things of Himself. Then, just as the Scriptures describe, all His attributes become a living person in us—God Himself.

This is the path we are on, and we will not settle for less. He has encouraged us with the vision of becoming "*one as we are one,*"[112] just as Jesus: "*I in them and you in me, all being perfected into one—so that the world will know that you sent me and will understand that you love them as much as you love me.*"[113]

Shalom.

---

109   Psalm 103:8b (KJV).

110   Romans 5:5b (NIV).

111   Hebrews 2:10 (KJV).

112   John 17:22 (NIV).

113   John 17:23 (TLB).

19.
I AM NOT SATISFIED!

EVER SINCE THE FALL, MANKIND SEEMS TO HAVE AN INSATIABLE DESIRE FOR knowledge. We are told that there is a space exploration program to land a man on Mars in 2025 that has been forty years in the making. The E.U. is spending multiple billions on an experiment (the supercollider) in order to create the circumstances they believe will hopefully prove the origins of the universe, better known as the "Big Bang Theory."

Mankind appears to never be satisfied with what we know or have experienced, so we invest our lives in exploring and discovering. But why? From a purely pragmatic standpoint, these adventures seem pointless compared to the need to solve the problems of poverty and disease that fill our world.

Genesis has the answer. In the beginning, mankind was refused the opportunity to eat from the tree of life because we couldn't resist the fruit of the tree of the knowledge of good and evil.[114] We can never be satisfied. We crave more and more knowledge, thinking this will finally bring conclusion to "the why of everything."

This same drive has consumed us in the spiritual realm. Humans are "gods-worshipping" creatures, ever searching for the "whys of life." Even we Christians are on a continual search for more knowledge of God than we have already encountered. The original purpose was for us to eat from the tree of life; from that position, the tree of knowledge would have its final conclusion in God Himself. It is only when we find the God of the tree of life that we can properly start this journey as God originally intended. This is the key to entering into all of God Himself, and it's then that all of His creation takes a secondary place.

Like the Apostle Paul, I am driven *"to know* [Him and] *the power of his resurrection."*[115] I crave a deeper and more intimate relationship with Him, not just facts about Him. I love the Scripture, but it's the God of the Scripture I pursue. He has encouraged us to *"seek and you **will** find"*[116] (emphasis added). This is not a maybe or a possibility, but a *will find*! This is part of what we as a church are seeking; we're

---

114   Genesis 2:9.

115   Philippians 3:10 (N(V).

116   Matthew 7:7 (NIV).

like orphans in a desperate pursuit to find our birth parent, God. We have His genes, and when He reveals Himself to our search, we recognize the family likeness, even though we are distorted by our dead sin nature.

I cannot rest; I am not satisfied with what I know, read from scripture, or experience of Him. I know there is more, maybe more than eternity can reveal. Is this why I am not satisfied? My journey does not find its conclusion on earth with information about God but with an ongoing knowing. But there is good news—God, for His part, is also seeking us, so much so that He has done everything possible to bring us back to Him through the sacrifice and death of His Son, Jesus. He states in Ezekiel: *"I gave you my solemn oath and entered into covenant with you... and you became mine."*[117]

The thrill of the journey with Him is that the more diligently we seek Him, the more He reveals Himself to us. He unfolds to us His person and the aspects of His character. Jeremiah 29:13 states: *"And you will seek Me and find Me, when you search for Me with all your heart"* (NKJV).

This life is about Him. Heaven is not just a place—it happens to be the result of who He is. We find that the journey with all its twists and turns brings new delights of joy and peace, and we can say as in the Song of Songs, *"... when I found the one my heart loves. I held Him and would not let Him go ..."*[118]

He has made us for Himself, and it appears He has chosen to not be satisfied either until He has us for His own. How can we resist such a God? What a poor picture we have shared by our often mean representation of Him. David cries, *"I shall be satisfied, when I awake, with thy likeness."*[119]

Shalom.

---

117 Ezekiel 16:8b (NIV).

118 Song of Songs 3:4 (NIV).

119 Psalm 17:15b (KJV).

20.
THE BLAME GAME

THE OLDEST STORY IN THE WORLD DESCRIBES THE ORIGIN OF THE "BLAME GAME." If anyone wants to confirm the divine inspiration of the book of Genesis, then this would be one of those pieces of evidence. This narrative explains how we came to develop a relational behaviour that is repeated every day, everywhere, by every family, society, religion, and culture. We are all prone by our carnal nature to shift blame from ourselves to others for things for which we are responsible and guilty.

Two innocent people, a man and a woman, live in a perfect relationship with each other and with God. The story explains that God visits them *"in the cool of the day"*[120] to enjoy their company. But one day, in an instant, the relationship between the couple and God is breached when the serpent appears, convincing the woman to disobey God's specific instructions not to eat the fruit of the *"... the tree of the knowledge of good and evil, for when you eat of it you will surely die."*[121] She succumbs to the temptation and is seduced by the potential benefits of the forbidden fruit and then shares it with her husband. The outcome is disastrous, as both realize they are naked and now fear their daily visit from God.

The inevitable happens. God shows up and they hide in shame at the sudden realization of their complete nakedness. When God questions them as to their reason for hiding, the "blame game" begins. Adam excuses himself by saying, *"... the woman **you** put with me—**she** gave me some fruit from the tree, and I ate it"*[122] (emphasis added). Blame is shifted first to God and then to the woman. Similarly, when Eve is confronted, she accuses Lucifer; *"... The **serpent** deceived me, and I ate"*[123] (emphasis added). Both avoid responsibility.

There is a biblical principle that states that everything reproduces after its own kind, and as result of the rebellion of Adam and Eve, all mankind knows how to shift blame. I have spent many years involved in the business world, and we have

---

120   Genesis 3:8 (NIV).
121   Genesis 2:17 (NIV).
122   Genesis 3:12 (NIV).
123   Genesis 3:13b (NIV).

mastered the skill of blaming the person not available to defend themselves against the accusation.

We have recently been praying for a man with a brain tumour, but his mother complains, "It hasn't worked yet. We fasted and prayed, and God did not heal him yet." A husband added, "Why didn't God prevent the holocaust, the earthquake, the flood, the avalanche, or any crisis situation?" We humans need someone to blame, and often the accusing finger points to God. How we scream our complaints when we are falsely accused and cry "Unfair! Where is justice?"

The only sinless person who ever walked the earth was Jesus Christ. He was falsely accused and then murdered in cold blood. But who was to blame? The finger points at us all. Sin was birthed in the first couple, and it's been inherited by every human being who came after them. Mankind is to blame, because we have all taken of that tree of the knowledge of good and evil. How can we bear such blame? We are totally naked before God with no one to blame but ourselves. The sinless Christ was murdered totally naked on a wooden cross before God and man "to take the blame"—the guiltless for the guilty, the pure for the impure, the sinless for the sinner.

Life is unfair, cruel, and unjust, but God is not to blame. We are. It is all the consequence of Adam's sin, but God has provided the remedy by allowing His Son to take total blame for our failures and sins. What we must do is ask His forgiveness for all our misdeeds and accept responsibility for them, because He has mercifully paid the consequences on our behalf: *"For God caused Christ, who Himself knew nothing of sin, actually to be sin for our sakes, so that in Christ we might be made good with the goodness of God."*[124] Jesus took the blame for us.

Shalom.

21.
HOME COOKING—PART 1

GOD HAS BLESSED ME WITH A WIFE WHO IS A REMARKABLE COOK … SO MUCH SO that eating out is not even a close second to her culinary skills. I go directly to the table of good food. She is concerned about content, health, and sometimes even the right-sized portion. Restaurant food can be exotic, but who knows whether or not there is too much salt, sugar, or spices, so even in an "eating out" culture, my over-whelming preference is *home cooking*. It occurred to me that spiritual food follows the same pattern; I can either dine on insights from other Christians or receive my food directly from God Himself (home cooking). I find I prefer to "eat at home."

In the search to become more like Christ, I was asking God how Jesus was able to do only what He saw the Father doing and say only what He heard the Father say. I wanted to know how He developed this depth of intimacy. From our present understanding of His relationship with God, I have no doubt that there will be a list of theological reasons that would challenge even the concept of having this sort of personal intimacy. Historically the church has isolated Jesus from us through the introduction of Mary, the saints, the clergy, or even the Bible itself. Consequently, they have made Him so inaccessible that Jesus is now a mystery to us, but the fact is, He is only too willing to "eat with me." *"Here I am! I stand at the door and knock. If anyone opens the door, I will come in and eat with that person, and they with me."*[125]

The quest is then: Can we know by experience the sort of "oneness" that Jesus experienced with the Father? Why bother even asking the question? One reason is that we are told to be like Him; we are to be "Christs" on earth and corporately as His bride. The standard is set extremely high, and since it was God who set the standard, it makes sense to ask Him how to reach it. The Scripture is full of jewels hidden in a field, but the onus is on us to seek out those gems and find them. God is not playing a game of hide and seek with us, but He's giving us revelation of Himself and His ways, and He has given us some ground rules to follow.

These truths are so precious that unless we have a pure heart, a teachable, hum-ble spirit, and perseverance to discover them, they can destroy us. Like the tree of

---

125   Revelation 3:20 (NIV).

life in the Garden of Eden, partaking when driven by the tree of the knowledge of good and evil is an eternal destiny not to be entertained.

Pure hearts, humility, and perseverance are the keys, but God has promised that He will help us, as John describes in his first letter to the churches:

> Yet I know that the touch of the His Spirit never leaves you, and you don't really need a human teacher. You know that his Spirit teaches you about all things. Remember that His teaching urges you to live in Christ, so that if He were suddenly to reveal Himself, we should still know exactly where we stand and should not have to shrink away."[126]

Yes, we need teachers, but they are to show us how to do home cooking and not depend on restaurant food, because we don't know all the ingredients in food cooked outside the home! We have made teaching about God a paid profession, and we have been enticed to eat their fare, but God wants us to enjoy His table directly: "*You prepare a table before me in the presence of my enemies.*"[127] Their role is like the parent who patiently instructs the child how get the food in its mouth and not in the hair or on the table, floor, walls, or even the parent's face! He has placed in the church gifts and ministries to help us and bring us to personal maturity:

> So Christ himself gave the apostles, the prophets, the evangelists, the pastors and teachers, to equip his people for works of service, so that the body of Christ may be built up until we all reach unity in the faith and in the knowledge of the Son of God and become mature, attaining to the whole measure of the fullness of Christ."[128]

Let's learn how to feed ourselves from the Master's table directly and not be totally dependent on restaurant food, even if we have wonderful food from the "five-fold ministry."

Shalom.

---

126 J.B. Phillips, *Letters to Young Churches: A Translation of the New Testament Epistles* (London: Geoffrey Bless, 1954), 212.

127 Psalm 23:5a (NIV).

128 Ephesians 4:11–13 (NIV).

22.
HOME COOKING—PART 2: THE APPLICATION

LEARNING TO GO DIRECTLY TO GOD HAS ALWAYS BEEN SOMETHING OF A challenge for the church, and this has created a variety of barriers via church doctrine as well as ourselves. We have developed diverse methods of hearing from God: We consult the Bible by randomly opening it and placing our finger on the page. We use promise boxes, ask prophets, pray to Mary or the saints, but *do not go directly to God Himself*. Jesus, by contrast, went directly to His Father. What are we missing?

You may argue, "Well, Jesus was the sinless Son of God, so He had no barriers." But what would you say if you discovered that Jesus had the same challenge as ourselves? The New Testament reveals that Jesus lived out His earthly ministry as "the Son of Man."

> *Let Christ himself be your example as to what your attitude should be. For he, who had always been God's by nature ... **stripped himself of all privilege** by consenting to be a slave by nature and being born as mortal man. And, having become man, he humbled himself by living a life of utter obedience, even to the extent of dying, and the death he died was the death of a common criminal.*[129] (emphasis added)

You will recall that Jesus had to persuade John to baptize Him. John knew that Jesus was the sinless second Adam, and it was confirmed when the Holy Spirit filled Him after He arose from the water. When all the people were being baptized, Jesus was baptized too, but as He was praying, the heaven was opened, and the Holy Spirit descended on Him in bodily form like a dove. Then a voice came from heaven: "*You are my Son, whom I love; with you I am well pleased.*"[130] Just as we do, Jesus needed the power of the Holy Spirit in order to fulfil His ministry. Based on this relationship, He could say; "*... I do nothing on My own initiative, but I speak these things the Father*

---

129 Philippians 2:5–8 (PHILLIPS).
130 Luke 3:22b (NIV).

has taught Me."[131] He prayed: "*... that they may be one as we are one—I in them and you in me ...*"[132]

"*You can never please God without faith, without depending on him,*"[133] writes the author of Hebrews, and because God said of His Son "I am well pleased," we can assume that the relationship Jesus had with His Father was by faith. If Jesus the sinless Son of God had to walk by faith, can we not conclude that we need to do the same? But you say, "Jesus was the perfect Son of God and was sinless; therefore, He has an advantage." This is true in that He had no inherent sin nature, but Jesus also said of us; "*... they will do even greater things than these, because I am going to the Father.*"[134]

He Himself shared fully in our experience of temptation, except He never sinned: "*For by virtue of His own suffering under temptation He is able to help those who are exposed to temptation.*"[135] Because of His victory in this realm, He became the perfect substitute for our sin. He provided for us through His death and resurrection access into the very presence of God: "*Let us therefore approach the throne of grace with fullest confidence, that we may receive mercy for our failures and grace to help in the hour of need.*"[136] There are no barriers between God and us other than the ones we erect by our faithlessness or habitual sin.

The psalmist states of the one who loves God: "*He will **call** on me, and I **will** answer him...*"[137] (emphasis added). This is God's reassurance that we can go directly to Him. God wants this type of relationship, because we were made for this kind of fellowship with Him.

How then do we know what God is saying if we do not hear a voice or see with our eyes what He is doing? This is where faith and the example of Jesus come into play. His walk with God was by faith, so we, by faith, must believe that if we ask God a question, He will answer.

I have developed some methods of my own. For most of my life, I have been guilty of asking something of God then expecting His response to be via a scripture that may occur ten weeks later, through circumstances, or "fleeces," or through confirmation by messages I hear ... and so on it goes. All these are good and valid, but

---

131   John 8:28b.
132   John 17:22b–23a (NIV).
133   Hebrews 11:6a (TLB).
134   John 14:12b (NIV).
135   Hebrews 2:18b (PHILLIPS).
136   Hebrews 4:16 (PHILLIPS).
137   Psalm 91:15 (KJV).

I don't think Jesus walked this way. He is our model and pattern for relationship to God and living the Christian life, so it follows that we need to abide by His example.

This may not fit your present doctrine, but I believe God wants us to do just as Jesus did and "go to God directly," expecting Him to answer what we have asked. He may speak some word instantly to our mind and spirit, a conversation with God, *"face to face"*[138] as He did with Moses.

How then do we check whether what we believe we hear is from God and not from ourselves or Satan? Jesus stated: *"My sheep listen to my voice …"*[139] We need to cultivate the language of heaven by saturating our minds with the scripture; *"Don't let the world around you squeeze you into its mould, but let God re-mould your minds from within …"*[140] The best way is to read His love letter and memorize it so that we can also judge what we hear from the scripture. Paul instructs the church in Corinth to "judge" the words of prophecy-based encouragement, revelation of spiritual things, messages from God, or teaching. This, however, is not the total scope of words from God. We must be open for God to share things with us that appear to be "out of the box," but this is for another teaching …

Shalom.

---

138   Exodus 33:11 (KJV).
139   John 10:27 (NIV),
140   Romans 12:2b (PHILLIPS).

23.
DOES GOD SMILE OR LAUGH?

I RECENTLY SAW A PAINTING OF THE LAST SUPPER WHERE JESUS AND THE apostles were all laughing. It was delightful and such a contrast to how we have sanitized our view of God. My reaction to the picture was to burst into a smile … smiling is contagious, as is laughing. But the question becomes: Does God smile or laugh, or is this just making God into our image? We only have two options as Christians: either we are made in the image of God, or we make God into the image of man.

The Toronto Blessing was and is famous for the manifestation of laughing. Some have interpreted it as demonic, but I can't believe demons can have such enjoyment. Others say it's all about emotion, but so is watching your favourite movie or sports event. Others say, "How can this be of God? It is so irreverent." But our view of what is reverent is distorted because it's based on our own experience and cultural background. Those of us who have encountered the pleasure of laughter in this experience will attest to its validity.

There is a new release regarding the praise and worship of God: "… *in thy presence is fullness of joy; at thy right hand there are pleasures for evermore.*"[141] In the book of Zephaniah, scripture further states:

> *For the Lord your God has arrived to live among you. He is a mighty Savior. He will give you victory. He will rejoice over you with great gladness; he will love you and not accuse you. Is that a joyous choir I hear? No, it is the Lord exulting over you in happy song.*[142]

Do you think that God might have had a smile on His face when He said, "… *This is my beloved Son, in whom I am well pleased*"?[143] Or have you considered that God might express the same pride over His kids as we do over ours when they achieve a reward for skating, top grades at school, or just look so beautiful? Do you think He is emotionless when He states, "… *Well done, thou good and faithful servant:*

---

141 Psalm 16:11 (KJV).

142 Zephaniah 3:17–18 (TLB).

143 Matthew 3:17 (KJV).

thou hast been faithful over a few things, I will make you ruler over many things: enter into the joy of thy lord"?[144] "He was so pleased with Enoch that He took him straight to His presence, and as for David, God said, "... *I have found David the son of Jesse, a man after my Heart, who will do all My will."*[145] How do you picture God's face in all of these instances?

As a son I wanted, above everything else, to please my father. I wanted his endorsement, but now my desire is to have God's smile of approval. Mothers smile with delight as they hold their newborns in their arms, but even if our parents reject us, the psalmist states: *"When my father and mother forsake me, then the Lord will take me up."*[146]

As I shared with a Christian friend how I have seen the wonder of God's ultimate plan for us to become one with Him, I felt the thrill God has in revealing Himself to us. The following morning as I meditated on the experience, I sensed God smiling at me, but as I looked again, His smile turned to laughter. I thought at first that He was amused by me, so I asked Him, "Are you laughing at me?" But He replied, "I am not laughing at you, I am laughing with you." God was taking pleasure in my pleasure, and just like the true Father that He is, we were enjoying our fellowship together. Jesus prayed, "... *that they might be one as we are one* ..."[147]

I sensed His favour and His smile and we laughed together—God and man, and only because of what Jesus has done. This is God "outside the box." If it wasn't for others having similar encounters, I would be concerned that I was fantasizing about God's outward display of His love and favour toward me.

Shalom.

---

144   Matthew 25:21 (KJV).
145   Acts 13:22
146   Psalm 27:10 (KJV).
147   John 17:22b (NIV).

24.
THE SECOND ADAM

God's plan for His creation and for man as outlined in Genesis was to be implemented through Adam: "*Then God* [Elohim] *said, 'Let us make mankind in our image, in our likeness ...'*"[148] This was so he could have fellowship with Him and rule the earth as God's representative. The rest is "history," as they say, with Eve being seduced by the serpent, and Adam following her lead in eating from the tree of the knowledge of good and evil. Adam was disobedient to God's instructions.

Banished from the real goal—to eat of the tree of life—meant that God's plan had been frustrated before it even got off the ground. With the exception of God's intervention by sending the Holy Spirit to impregnate a young Virgin Mary, the failure of the son of God, Adam, and his wife, Eve, has been reproduced in every human being since that experience. The breakdown of the first Adam required a qualified second Adam to not only fulfill God's intent for man's original destiny, but also to clean up the mess left by the original Adam's sin.

The main thrust of the incarnation plan was to cut the "sin gene" that had infected the human race, pay for the consequences of that sin, and impregnate the Adamic race with the same Holy Spirit who enabled the second Adam to live a sinless life. The second Adam was to face the same testing and challenges as the first. Mankind was trapped by the failure of the original Adam, and if the second was to author the plan of redemption for the human race, He had to succeed where the first Adam failed.

The playing field had to be level for justice to work; therefore, it was necessary for the second Adam (Jesus) to face the same type of temptations as the first one (Matthew 4:1–11; Hebrews 2:5–18). To achieve this goal, He had to not only divest Himself of all the privileges as Son of God, but He also had to become the "Son of Man" (Philippians 2:6–7) and subject Himself to all the temptations and challenges faced by mankind. Even though Jesus was sinless, He identified with fallen humanity by persuading John the Baptist to baptize Him for the "repentance of sins." This pleased God (Matthew 3:17), who then equipped Him with same Holy Spirit who was given to all who believed in the rescue operation. Furthermore, He was required

---

148 Genesis 1:26 (NIV).

to depend on walking by faith in relationship with his Father, just as we are: "*And without faith it is impossible to please Him.*"[149] If He was to accomplish the rescue mission for mankind, He needed to face all the challenges of life as a human being (John 1:14; Hebrews 2:5–18), including our human learning process from a baby, to a child, (Luke 2:46), to an adult. The Holy Spirit gifted Him with the same gifts available to redeemed mankind. He stated that He only said what the Father told Him to say (word of knowledge, word of prophecy—John 12:50) and only did what He saw the Father doing (gifts of healing and miracles—John 5:19). He therefore became the perfect sacrifice to atone (pay) for all the sins of Adam's children.

Where Adam had failed by disobeying God's instructions, Jesus was obedient to the Father in everything, even having to die a criminal's death (Philippians 2:5–11). In the Garden of Gethsemane, His humanity (Son of Man) cried out to God, appealing for an alternative way for this part of the rescue operation. Nevertheless, He completed His obedience by stating, "*... not my will, but yours be done.*"[150] His obedience to His Father not only "wiped the slate clean" for the human race, but it also defeated the devil, who had seduced the first Adam.

Jesus, as the second Adam, succeeded in everything, bringing salvation to all mankind, (Hebrews 5:7), whereas the first Adam only succeeded in bringing death and disaster to everyone and everything.

Because Jesus is our role model, mentor, saviour, and Lord, we can be encouraged to live, walk, and talk as He did. Since He stated, "*greater things than these*"[151] we would do, we can be assured that He wasn't giving us a task too high to reach or too far to go. As the people of God, we have exactly the same promises and equipping to do the Father's work ... but even this is not the end. The original plan was dominion over creation (Earth) and fellowship with God, but now it becomes reigning with Him in the new heavens and new earth and *becoming one with him...*

Shalom.

---

149   Hebrews 11:6.

150   Luke 22:42 (NIV).

151   John 5:20 (NIV).

25.
ANTI-CHRISTIAN ERA

RECENT ONTARIO LEGISLATION IMPLEMENTING THE TEACHING OF SEX education in all Catholic and public schools indicates an anti-Christian bias. Moreover, this course forces all teachers, beginning in Grade One, to apply the curriculum, even if it is against their moral or religious beliefs. From the presentation I saw, all forms of sexual expression will be taught to innocent children who are not mature enough to receive such information. One must assume that the agenda of the architects of such a program is to create a sexual climate normalizing all forms of sexual behaviour. This clearly exposes the prejudice against the one taught in the Judeo-Christian culture.

The Law Society of Ontario and other societies across Canada have petitioned governments to ban law graduates of Trinity Western Christian University from practicing in any province because of a "Christian sexual moral behaviour code" they signed while attending university. Nova Scotia's position has been challenged and defeated because it was deemed to break the "freedom of religion" clause in the Canadian charter. The fact that numerous large business organizations are supporting the planned ban on Christian graduates illustrates yet another facet of society participating in the existing, ever increasing anti-Christian climate.

I have challenged my own bank (BMO) at the highest levels, and their response was that they are "inclusive" of all sexual behaviours, yet their stand against Christian law graduates proves they are in fact "excluding" those with a Christian moral view of sexual behaviour.

The City of Toronto has established a by-law making it almost impossible for new church buildings to be erected. Those Christians who cannot afford a building but rent school property have been given an 800 per cent rent increase. For example, rent has increased from $5,673 a year to $44,695, making the rental of public school property impossible for churches. At the same time, Islamic students are allowed to use a school cafeteria absolutely free for Friday prayers. The "Christianised" Western world has moved goal posts from being "post-Christian" to "anti-Christian." Case in point—the head of religious broadcasting at Britain's BBC is a Muslim.

The religious and social consequences of society moving against the moral codes revealed in the Scripture will be devastating. We need only look at the consequences of Israel's fall from grace into idolatry to see the slippery slope on which today's culture is now sliding. History tells us that civilizations are corrupted from within, and Western culture is no exception. Islam is poised to fill the moral vacuum with law that is barbaric, brutal, cruel, and, if permitted, will return us to "the dark ages."

What then should we do as Christians? What is our responsibility toward our society as it becomes increasingly anti-Christian? Should we form a political party and fight this out in the political arena, or is there another way? Although all this sounds like bad news, there is a bright side. Because this world continues to plunge deeper into moral darkness, it is now that the people of God have an opportunity to let the real light be seen. Jesus said that not only is He "the light of the world," but we are too.[152] A single candle shining in a totally dark night can be seen up to fifteen miles away. The darker it gets, the brighter the light will appear.

God is refining His church, cleaning the spots and ironing out the wrinkles from His bride (the *ecclesia*, the "called out ones") in preparation for the wedding of His Son. Our call is to prepare for the return of our Bridegroom and at the same time let our lives reveal the Kingdom of God to the world. *"But we know that when Christ appears, we shall be like him, for we shall see him as he is. All who have this hope in him* **purify themselves,** *just as he is pure"*[153] (emphasis added).

Light doesn't shine brightly out of a dirty lamp; the more transparent the glass, the greater the level of light emitted. We are to be Jesus' light of the world to the world around us. Because of the oppression caused by darkness, doing this will usher in an opportunity for a great harvest of mankind into the Kingdom of light.

"The people walking in darkness have seen a great light; on those living in the land of deep darkness a light has dawned."[154] We are to be that light.

Arise, shine, for your light has come, and the glory of the Lord rises upon you. See, darkness covers the earth and thick darkness is over the peoples, but the Lord rises upon you and his glory appears above you. Nations will come to your light, and kings to the brightness of your dawn.[155]

Shalom.

---

152   John 8:12.
153   1 John 3:2–3 (NIV).
154   Isaiah 9:2 (NIV).
155   Isaiah 60:1–3 (NIV).

26.
WHOM CAN WE TRUST?

DURING A RECENT PRAYER MEETING, A COMMENT WAS MADE AFFIRMING someone for whom we were praying with the phrase, "There are very few people I can trust, and you are one of them." It was meant as a special relationship word of encouragement, but it exposed a fundamental issue of human behaviour—that of trust.

Why do we need to "trust," and why is that trust so often betrayed? For society to function with some degree of success requires each of us do what we say we will do and be what we should be for others. I have to trust that others on the road will obey the rules of the road, that they will stop at red lights and only go on green ones. When the sign states "walk," I trust that those in cars will obey the signs. Having spent some time in China and other parts of Asia, I've discovered that these rules do not fully apply. A red light often means "only if you have to stop." Green means "go if you can," and walk means taking your life into your own hands!

All business life functions on degrees of trust, and all social, recreational, and family life is the same. The "Christianized" parts of the world exercise higher levels of trust and success as societies because the belief and value system of the Judeo-Christian ethic influences behaviour.

Trust betrayed cuts deeply into our personal lives, and we can easily develop a "fortress" mentality against everything and anyone. We can be imprisoned by the betrayal of big business, governments, churches, clergy, family, and even those as close as brothers, sisters, and parents. The deepest hurts, wounds, and damage often come from our own flesh and blood. Those closest to us are the means of both our security and our destruction.

Despite all of these disappointments, we have a deep need to trust. As human beings we are not self sufficient. We are created gregarious, which means we need and want others. Likewise, we were made to know and trust God, but many feel they cannot trust Him either. Some life experience fills them with disappointment, and God gets the blame: Why did my son have to die so young? Why did God allow the Holocaust?

We are both the victims and the cause of betrayal of trust. None of us are innocent, and the reason lies in the original failure to trust exercised by our first parents. Adam and Eve failed to trust what God had said about eating from the tree of the knowledge of good and evil. They crossed traffic on a "red" light. We have all since reproduced the same traffic violation. We are guilty of disobedience and "T-boning" each other at the intersections of life.

God has revealed a solution to our dilemma. Despite the fact that we often do not trust Him, He has taken the initiative to demonstrate His love. He became the victim for all situations of betrayal of trust. The writer of Hebrews states: "… [He] *has been tempted in every way, just as we are* …"[156] He was betrayed and abandoned by his disciples, and even as He was being murdered unjustly, He cried in apparent despair at God's abandonment: "*My God, my God, why have you forsaken me?*"[157] He has walked where we walk, and He knows the anguish better than us all.

"So what?" we ask. This proves that even Jesus suffered the same as we do. The beauty of Jesus is that in the betrayal and abandonment, He shows us the way out. He gives us the keys to set us free so that life's experiences do not become chains that bind us. One of the last recorded words from the cross was, "*Father forgive them, for they do not know what they are doing.*"[158] Jesus spoke these words in reference to those who had unjustly murdered Him. We are both those who are murdered and also the murderers, and the key out of the prison for murderers is to forgive those who murder us. This may be the greatest challenge of our lives, because the pain, the hurt, is so deep, and we want justice too!

Jesus taught us a very simple but incredibly profound prayer, which contains these words: "*… and forgive us our sins, just as we have forgiven those who have sinned against us.*"[159] The only part of the Lord's Prayer He chose to explain was that our heavenly Father will forgive us if we forgive those who sin against us, but if we refuse to forgive them, He will not forgive us.[160] Failure to forgive locks us in a prison of our own unforgiveness, forever and ever and ever …

Still troubled by the need for justice? God, as a God of incredible mercy and forgiveness, states, "*It is mine to avenge; I will repay.*"[161] He will balance the books. Leave justice in the hands of God, who sees and knows the hearts of both the victim and the victimizer.

Shalom.

---

156   Hebrews 4:15 (NIV).

157   Mark 15:34b (NIV).

158   Luke 23:34 (NIV).

159   Matthew 6:12 (NIV).

160   Matthew 6:14–16.

161   Romans 12:19b (NIV).

27.
A RUSHING MIGHTY WIND

MY VISION: IT WAS AT THE END OF A RECENT PRAYER MEETING THAT I HEARD and saw the effects of a gale force wind as it entered the church building at the western front and then in a nanosecond rushed out through the rear wall. Though there were no people in the church at the time, the wind took everything with it, emptying the place even more. Such was the force of the wind that I saw branches falling from trees, and leaves being ripped from the branches, then strangely, a calm stillness as the wind disappeared toward the east.

I was aware that I was an observer of this experience, just as John was in the book of Revelation. The word that came to me was, "I am cleansing; I am purging my church, and nothing will be able to withstand the power of that wind." It was like the breath of God, but this time the breath was not giving life but purifying the church of all that defiles, all that is dead, all that is lifeless, and nothing could stand the tremendous force of His breath. Though the building was shaken, it remained intact but totally empty. I saw no people but wondered what the vision of falling tree branches with leaves being stripped could mean, so I followed the Apostle John's example and asked the Lord.

This is what I was given to understand: The leaves being forcibly removed from the branches by the breath of God was the removal of all man's efforts and plans to build his church by his own understanding, and this was being removed by force. All the natural works of man, as good as they may appear, will be removed by the coming move of God. The temple will be cleansed by God Himself. Nothing unholy or the works of man will remain or defile in the Holy place of God's dwelling.

We are in the season of God preparing the bride for the wedding supper of the Lamb and the New Jerusalem so that He can dwell with man forever. We will experience demonstrations of God's mighty power, but nothing will be able to stand before it except the pure in heart, kept *"in the cleft of the rock"*[162] as the wind passes by them.

---

162 Exodus 33:22.

The Apostle John appeals to the church: *"All who have this hope in him purify themselves, just as he is pure."*[163] The warning to us is that failure to purify ourselves will expose us to God's wind of purification; the judgement seat of Christ talks of our lives not only producing gold, silver, and precious stones, but also wood, hay, and stubble. God's wind is to purge the church now so that we will not be blown away with that "mighty rushing wind."

Shalom.

---

163 1 John 3:3 (NIV).

28.
MYOPIA

ACCORDING TO *WEBSTER'S NEW WORLD DICTIONARY*, MYOPIA IS DEFINED AS "abnormal vision, objects not seen clearly." Have you ever heard the phrase, "They look at life through rose-coloured glasses"? This condition is common to us all—not that we only view or understand life as through *rose-coloured* glasses, but rather by our very nature we distort everything we see and hear. It's a direct consequence of our inherited sin nature. This sin nature has turned us from being God-centred to self-centred, resulting in all of our experiences being coloured from the perspective of self.

Because self is front and centre, we cannot experience a clear view of anything, particularly each other. A case in point: I was leading a meeting with a colleague and thought I clearly saw his shortcomings as well as those of others, but in the eyes of some, I failed to see my own. This now leads us to the heart of the issue. Was I correct, or were they? If guilty, are we prepared to admit our failures and learn from each other?

We might then ask as did Pilate of Jesus, "*What is truth?*"[164] In light of the fact that all of us see to varying degrees of distortion, can we ever reach a full understanding of truth, or with each other? There is an inherent disconnect between us all, which appears to be an unbridgeable gap. How can we see clearly and communicate the truth if our hearing receptors and vision are so distorted?

Enough questions. The answers originate in the failure of both Adam and Eve. They listened to a distorted understanding of God by the tempter himself; "*Did God really say... ?*"[165] He suggested that God was withholding the full truth from them, and that lie has distorted our understanding of the very nature of God Himself as well as our relationship with Him.

God has taken the initiative to restore clear vision through Jesus Christ, who stated, "*I am the Light of the world.*"[166] But you might ask how we can see clearly because of this light. Jesus told a university graduate in theology the following: "...

---

164   John 18:38a (NIV).

165   Genesis 3:1 (NIV).

166   John 8:12.

*Very truly I tell you, **no one can see** the kingdom of God, unless they born again*"[167] (emphasis added). We need to start from a new God-centred position to be able to see ourselves and life clearly. Viewing life from only a position in the valley is very different to seeing things from the mountain top.

The priority for us then is learning to see life from God's point of view until we behave like Jesus, who only did what He saw the Father doing. The pattern is set out for us in the Scripture as follows:

1. Recognize that we all suffer the effects of the sin nature, which causes myopia.
2. Repent of the sin caused by our blindness to both God and others.
3. Become humble enough to admit we need God's help, even if it comes via others.
4. Desire a pure heart with no self-centred agendas: *"Blessed are the pure in heart, for they will see God."*[168]
5. Accept God's grace to "*... walk not after the flesh, but after the Spirit.*"[169]
6. Be "*led by the Spirit of God*"[170] and not by our carnal nature.
7. Manifest "*the fruit of the Spirit.*"[171]

One of the worst forms of myopia occurs in religion, and I include Christianity under this generic umbrella. Unless we are prepared to see what we believe from God's revelation and not ours, we murder those who oppose our understanding. Jesus is the classic case of the ultra- religious attempting to kill truth by killing the purveyor of it. Regrettably, this is also the history of the church. Catholics believed they were justified in burning Protestants for heresy.

Protestants in turn drowned Anabaptists because they believed in total immersion, not sprinkling. Some Baptists consider Charismatics to be demon possessed, and so on it goes. Even our local churches are not immune from the disease of myopia. In fact, this article is a direct result of this very experience. That is why we need to walk in the Spirit, be led by the Spirit, produce the fruit of the Spirit, and walk in the unity of the Spirit.

Shalom.

---

167 John 3:3 (NIV).
168 Matthew 5:8 (NIV).
169 Romans 8:1 (KJV).
170 Romans 8:14 (KJV).
171 Galatians 5:22 (KJV).

29.
WHO ARE WE DOING IT FOR?

I RECALL AN EXPERIENCE THAT HAPPENED TO MY FAVOURITE BIBLE TEACHER OF the 1970s and 80s, Bob Mumford. He pastored a church that had entered into a new building construction program. The men of the church had agreed to start digging the foundations one Saturday morning, and Bob had decided to become part of the team. As the morning wore on, men gradually faded from the workforce, and at one point he looked up to find only himself in the "trenches."

He immediately complained to God: "But I am the pastor. I am God's man of faith and power. Why am I left to do digging?" The "man of faith and power" bit was added tongue in cheek as he told the story. The reply came back immediately; "And *who do you think you are doing it for?*"

For the local church to function as God intends requires that we view God as our "employer," and our attitude toward the work of God demands we do it unto Him. There will always be situations that challenge our motives regarding our faithfulness, perseverance, and consistency in order to test who we are doing it for! Paul encourages slaves to work for their masters "as unto God," and not just the good ones but the ones that are cruel, mean, and harsh. He then quotes the attitude of Christ in His response to false accusations and the planned murder of Himself.

Every community activity will have as much tension as there are people on the team. Sports teams rise and fall on attitude more than skill. Businesses spiral to destruction as a result of internal personality conflicts. Churches split over "*I am of Paul*" and "*I of Apollos*" and "*I of Cephas*" and "*I of Christ*"[172] as well as inconsequential issues of doctrine, but the majority is over things that are grounded in wrong attitudes.

I know of situations in the past where this church has almost self destructed because we have ignored God's pattern of working together. This is not my church, and it's not yours either. It is Christ's, and we are the body of Christ. If we want things our own way, then we become a cancer in the system ... and all cancers die once they kill the host.

As we grow from strength to strength by God's grace and blessing, we must keep this clearly in our focus: this is His church, and all we do, or fail to do, we do

---

172   1 Corinthians 1:12.

for Him or to Him. All offences we face are to test *"Who are we doing it for?"* We must face all rejections, failures, mistakes, false accusations, and lies with the same attitude. We need to be fast "on the draw" to forgive because we are all failures. Jesus said, *"But if you do not forgive others their sins, your Father will not forgive your sins."*[173] We are all tarred with same brush. The church is composed of sinners—the only difference is that we are sinners saved by grace. God is determined that we be conformed to the image of His Son. The question is: Can we stand the test?

Our eternal end is glorious. We will be *like* Him, we will be *one* with Him, and we will *reign* with Him. Let us put life's experience into this eternal context. To get there, we have to follow the pattern of our Lord. Let's ask God to help us see things from His perspective and surrender to His process of being conformed into the image of His Son.

> *In your relationships with one another, have the same mindset as Christ Jesus: Who, being in very nature God, did not consider equality with God something to be used to his own advantage; rather, he made himself nothing by taking the very nature of a servant, being made in human likeness. And being found in appearance as a man, he humbled himself by becoming obedient to death— even death on a cross! Therefore God exalted him to the highest place and gave him the name that is above every name, that at the name of Jesus every knee should bow, in heaven and on earth and under the earth, and every tongue acknowledge that Jesus Christ is Lord, to the glory of God the Father."*[174]

Shalom.

---

173   Matthew 6:15 (NIV).
174   Philippians 2:5–11 (NIV).

30.
NOT DRESSED FOR THE OCCASION

HAVE YOU EVER ARRIVED AT AN EVENT ONLY TO FIND THAT YOU HAD MISJUDGED the type of clothing you should be wearing? I conducted an outdoor wedding in Ganaraska Forest last year and assumed that the dress code would reflect the natural surroundings. Much to my surprise, it was a full "shirt and tie" event, with women in very high heels and full wedding gear. I scrambled to arrange my attire in order to look dressed for the occasion, but being tieless, I decided to do up the top button on my white shirt so I would look like a preacher from the Reformed church!

Similarly, dressed in my PJ's one morning, my prayer commenced with, "Good morning, Lord," but it hadn't occurred to me that I might not be "dressed for the occasion" of being in the presence of the holiest One of all eternity. Suddenly, I was aware not of my PJ's, but of my casual words of introduction. Was I too familiar? Was I being less than respectful of God? I looked into my heart and saw no disrespect, only that God made Himself available at my level of relationship. Jesus, as Son of Man, has made this possible for us all.

I was, however, aware of my uncleanness—not of any particular sin, but as a human being with an old sinful nature. I endeavour to keep *"a pure heart"*[175] before God, so this experience revealed the great gap between natural man and a Holy God. This seemed a paradox to me. On the one hand I was relaxed in His presence, talking with Him "face to face" as friends, while on the other hand I was aware of my uncleanness, even though it appeared not to hinder our personal encounter. Remembering the complex process and requirements laid out in the Old Covenant, I should be grovelling on my face before God, yet here I was in my PJ's talking with Him face to face.

At this point, the prosecuting attorney (the accuser of the brethren) read me a list of my failures, sins, and faults, screaming that I was guilty. My only reply was to agree with his statement: guilty as charged. But I felt no condemnation, only a gentle peace that enveloped me. That was my advocate, my defence counsel, declaring that all charges against me had been dismissed and paid for; I am forgiven! Although I could not see it with the natural eye, it was then that I realized I was covered from

---

175   Psalm 24:4 (KJV).

head to toe with a pure-white garment, making me as pure as the Son of Man Himself. I was at home with Father, just like Jesus, and I could enjoy the same face-to-face relationship with the Father as He did.

I believe that the implications of this remarkable work of grace and love of God that Jesus accomplished for us through His life, death, and resurrection have yet to be fully understood, experienced, or acted upon. As a wretched man by nature, I can become one with God, all because of what Jesus has done for me; He has *dressed me for the occasion.*

Can I boast of this intimacy with God, this familiarity with the Almighty? Absolutely not! I am the beneficiary of this amazing love, and my heart cries out with the hymn writer: "Were the whole realm of nature mine, that were a present far too small, love so amazing so divine *demands*, my soul, my life, my all."[176] My reply is to say that He *shall* have my soul, my life, my all.

So here I am, dressed in my PJ's, a sinner saved by grace, talking face-to-face with the Father, just like Jesus.

Shalom.

---

176 "Selah Lyrics." *AZ Lyrics.* Accessed October 13, 2017. https://www.azlyrics.com/lyrics/selah/whenisurveythewondrouscross.html.

31.
IN A FOG?

When we lived in the U.K., the fall and winter would be plagued by dense fogs called "pea soupers." You could hardly see but a few feet in front of you. I recall commuting from London in my tiny shoebox-sized Morris Mini, and I could just see the front of the hood. I had to hang my head out the window to try and follow the curbs in the road. Fog is a natural phenomenon caused by the difference between ground and air temperatures, as well as the absence of wind, but fog in the U.K. is compounded by heavy air pollution (hence the phrase "pea soupers"), resulting in an extreme health hazard.

Recently during one of my morning prayer times, I seemed to be in one of those spiritual "pea soupers." It was as if I was surrounded by a dense mist that obscured God from my spiritual vision. The fog was so claustrophobic that all my senses were dead, and I couldn't see or hear. I felt smothered by the grey mist while craving the warmth and brightness of the sun and a fresh breeze on my face.

Some have experienced the "heavens as brass" issue, when prayer appears to rebound and God is but a distant thought. This I believe is a companion to the fog encounter I had. Admittedly I do not have a clear understanding of the reason, except for the principle that the natural is patterned after the spiritual. First, there is a "temperature difference" between heaven and my spirit. I may be spiritually cold. The solution lies in my desire for the "warmth and brightness of the Son." When I persevere to seek His face, my "body temperature rises" as the Holy Spirit increases my spiritual temperature. The more I continue coming closer to heaven's climate, the clearer my seeing and hearing. It doesn't matter how dense the fog. The sun continues to shine, and if we continue to seek, ask, and allow the wind of the Spirit to drive away the fog, we will see the Son shine.

The second, more difficult, challenge is getting rid of the pollution. This requires an honest review of our pattern of living. The more we continue to allow our sinful behaviour to pollute our lives, the denser the fog and greater the spiritual health hazard. "*Search me, O God, and know my heart: try me, and know my thoughts: And see if there be any wicked way in me, and lead me in the way everlasting*"[177] until we

---

177   Psalm 139:23–24 (KJV).

can pray, "*Let the words of my mouth, and the meditation of my heart, be acceptable in thy sight, O Lord, my strength, and my redeemer.*"[178]

Then of course there is the challenge of the limitations of our mortal bodies. As Paul states: "*Now all that I know is hazy and blurred, but then I will see everything clearly, just as clearly as God sees into my heart right now.*"[179] The tease, the frustration of it all, is having the knowledge that there is so much more but knowing we do not have the "eyes" to see clearly or possess the capacity to understand fully till that day. The writer to Hebrews tells us that we need to exercise faith to walk this life, so that even though at times it appears we're living life in a fog, the reality is that the sun is always shining beyond it: "*Now faith means putting our full confidence in the things we hope for, it means being certain of things we cannot see.*"[180]

One day the fog will lift, never to return, and we shall see Him face-to-face. All tears will be wiped away, and there will be no more sorrow, death, or pain, and God will dwell with us forever!

Shalom.

---

178   Psalm 19:14 (KJV).

179   1 Corinthians 13:12b (TLB).

180   Hebrews 11:1 (PHILLIPS).

32.
TOLERANCE VERSUS INTOLERANCE

MILITANT ISLAM AND MILITANT ATHEISM

MILITANT ISLAM. THE NEWLY-FORMED OFFSPRING OF ISIS ("THE ISLAMIC State") in Syria and Iraq has given all minority groups, including Christians, the option to convert to their version of Islam or die. They have circulated horrific pictures on the Internet showing the brutal killing of either Shia or minority groups.

Because historical Christian records are not free of similar intolerant actions toward other segments of the church or Muslims, it could be argued that, "… *He who is without sin among you, let him be the first to throw a stone at her*."[181] Can we then with a clear conscience now condemn ISIS?

The message of Christ and His true disciples is one of good news to all men with love, mercy, and forgiveness at its heart, but Islam's founder left instructions to kill the infidel and unbeliever. The spirit of the founders of each of these religions oppose one another, and the proof of it carries through to its disciples. What ISIS is doing is following the pattern set by Muhammad. When Christians have shown intolerance, murder, and hate, as in the Inquisition, they have *not* been following the life and teaching of Christ. It is from this standpoint that we can accuse some followers of Islam of brutal behaviour. They, for their part, are only acting in accordance with their beliefs.

All Western nations have an open and free society that is tolerant of all religious beliefs, but what is the consequence of allowing a religion that is intolerant of conflicting religions or lifestyles to flourish? We see the brutal reality of what happens to the tolerant when the intolerant, who are growing in number, are equipped with arms and money. Remember, most of the Middle East, North Africa, and Turkey were "Christianized" over a period of three hundred years. Islam, however, reversed that position with the sword in just thirty short years, and it has remained that way for 1,400 years. With the rate of Muslim immigration, and the high birth rate within that population, the numbers are against Western nations who are "tolerant" of all in their midst, including the Muslims. If this continues, the balance of "tolerance to intolerance" will shift with the numbers.

---

181 John 8:7b

As a child I lived through the Second World War, and my observation would be that there are things worse than war. This could be one of them. History is not on our side in the numbers game, and democracy has now become our enemy. Witness the Muslim Brotherhood experience in Egypt, and the anarchy in Libya, Somalia, Syria, Sudan, Yemen, and Nigeria. History also proves that you cannot fight an idea with military might, particularly a religious one.

What can we do as we face the potential of the intolerant consuming the tolerant? The normal answer would be to oppose it with a superior idea or religion. Christianity fits that role perfectly, but it seems as if the spirit behind Islam anticipated such a challenge, and in the Koran instructed the Muslim faithful to kill all apostates: "But if they turn back [from Islam] take [hold] of them wherever you find them" (Quran 4:89); "They have a curse on them; whenever they are found they shall be seized and slain [without mercy]" (Quran 33:57–61). Don't dare question, do not in any way defile the book or challenge the Koran, because that also carries the charge of blasphemy and a death sentence to the perpetrators. All bases are now covered, and the followers are trapped behind walls of control and the fear of death. What options do we have as societies and countries? Will we be engulfed by Islamic intolerance?

Militant Atheism. Militant atheism has declared war on all religions, particularly Christianity, and will not tolerate any form of belief that holds ideas contradicting their philosophy. Evolution, the atheists say, is "fact," and any who challenge this doctrine cannot hold public office. They intend to remove all reference to Christianity from our society, tax churches, stop all forms of public prayer, and deny the rights of doctors to abstain from performing abortions or, potentially, euthanasia.

We have heard all this before. Hitler, Stalin, Mao, and every dictator in history follows the same pattern of intolerance to anything or anyone challenging their philosophy or power. Both militant Islam and militant atheism come from the same source. It is the work of the destroyer, Lucifer himself.

It is time for the "church militant" to arise from its comfort zone and engage both of these enemies of God and His Christ, whether we are called to confront their intolerance in the political realm or with the weapons Paul outlines in Ephesians: *"For we wrestle not against flesh and blood, but against principalities, against powers, against the rulers of the darkness of this world, against spiritual wickedness in high places."*[182] As Christians we have "weapons of mass destruction and blessing" in prayer. We are told of the source of the power behind such evil; the Living Bible paraphrases the above text this way:

---

182 Ephesians 6:12 (KJV).

For we are not fighting against people made of flesh and blood, but against persons without bodies—evil rulers of the unseen world, those mighty satanic beings and great evil princes of darkness who rule this world; and against huge numbers of wicked spirits in the spirit world. So use every piece of God's armor to resist the enemy whenever he attacks, and when it is all over, you will be still standing up.[183]

"And pray in the Spirit on all occasions with all kinds of prayer and requests. With this in mind, be alert and always keep on praying for all the Lord's people."[184]

Shalom.

---

183   Ephesians 6:12–13 (TLB).

184   Ephesians 6:18 (NIV).

33.
PLEASURE AND PLEASING

FOR MUCH OF CHURCH HISTORY, WE HAVE WRESTLED WITH THE IDEA THAT pleasure is sinful. This has created a general picture of Christianity as being a "lemon juice" religion. We have worn black clothes, black looks, and spoken of doom, destruction, and judgement ... hardly the Good News of the Kingdom of God that Jesus talked about. Scripture clearly states: *"... in thy presence is fullness of joy; at thy right hand there are pleasures for evermore."*[185] It is in His presence that fullness of joy is found, but we pervert the most beautiful of life encounters when the end becomes the experience of pleasure alone. So what are we missing?

We have failed to understand that the correct experience of pleasure is that it is the consequence of our actions, not the pursuit of it for its own sake. Pleasure becomes our god when we desire it only for the "high" that it gives. What is worse is that it causes us to constantly seek satisfaction in a craving that is, by definition, insatiable.

Every addiction, perversion, and ambition has its root in making the experience of pleasure the reason for our actions rather than it being the fruit. Whether it is the taste buds on our tongues, the thrill of sex, or the "high" of drugs, all lead to the same end. The Rolling Stones described it best: "I can't get no satisfaction!" Even the highest and noblest of desires are subject to the same end. When we Christians judge spiritual experiences from the pleasure we receive from them, we pollute these too. There can be a very subtle twisting of our motives when we describe the worship service as "awesome" if we base it on the degree of pleasure we enjoy rather than the personal encounter with God.

We were created for His pleasure. When we focus on bringing Him pleasure, our motives can be pure. But as soon as we make our enjoyment level the focal point, we are in danger. The remarkable thing is that when we give pleasure, we also receive pleasure, and it is at this point that the opportunity comes to direct our focus on receiving rather than giving. Now how sneaky is that?

Some pleasures are enjoyed vicariously. Parents watch with delight as Johnny takes his first uncertain steps. God could not contain Himself when He loudly

---

185   Psalm 16:11 (KJV).

announced; *"... This is my beloved Son, in whom I am well pleased."*[186] In the movie *Chariots of Fire*, because his focus was on running in the Olympics for Britain, Eric Little is berated by his religious sister for not rushing off to China "to save souls." His reply was: "When I run, I feel His pleasure." God takes pleasure even in the delight we take in our achievements. Eric did go to China, saved souls, and died a martyr's death. One time I sensed God laughing at me, and when I asked why He was laughing, His reply was: "I am not laughing *at* you—I am laughing *with* you."

There is also a dark side to pleasing that can never be satisfied. There are those who demand that we always please them, and they use that reasoning as a basis for a relationship. This is not a foundation for healthy fellowship; it is control as well as a perversion, and it is how Satan runs his kingdom.

Setting ourselves to please God is the most noble of pursuits, as Paul states: *"It is our aim, therefore, to please him..."*[187] Can we say the same or do we seek the pleasure of worship rather than the One we worship? Pleasing God is not all sweet and light. It may well have a martyr's future, just like Eric Little. And then there's our Saviour ... looking ahead to the joy set before Him, Jesus endured the cross, despising the shame of it because it was His Father's will and He wanted to please Him. When pleasing God is the motive, then irrespective of the pain in the process, *"... joy cometh in the morning."*[188]

Let us set our hearts to please Him always, because He is worthy ... whether the "worship" we experience as awesome is judged by our degree of pleasure or not. The natural consequence of making God the centre of our affection is the blessing of His presence flowing like water from a spring to all those around us: *"But you will receive power when the Holy Spirit comes on you; and you will be my witnesses in Jerusalem, and in Judea and Samaria, and to the ends of the earth."*[189]

Shalom.

---

186   Matthew 3:17 (KJV).

187   2 Corinthians 5:9 (PHILLIPS).

188   Psalm 30:5b (KJV).

189   Acts 1:8 (NIV).

34.
THE EIGHTY-TWENTY PRINCIPLE

IT IS A COMMONLY UNDERSTOOD PRINCIPLE IN LIFE THAT THE DIVISION BETWEEN those who are actively achieving and those who are passive is proportionally divided into 80 per cent passive and only 20 per cent active. This principle is reflected in all walks of life, and regrettably also in the church. But should the world's norm apply to the body of Christ?

In light of Paul's biblical description of the human body as a representation of Christ's church, or "called out ones" (ecclesia), is the eighty-twenty pattern biblical or worldly? Looking at our own bodies as an example, our existence would be very limited if only 20 per cent was functioning (though on a more humorous note, we probably feel that way sometimes in our lives)! Paul states: "*Now here is what I am trying to say: **All** of you together are the one body of Christ, and **each one** of you is a separate and **necessary** part of it*"[190] (emphasis added).

Firstly, if we fail to play our part, then the whole body will be dysfunctional. If only 20 per cent are "playing their part," we have a totally malfunctioning church … welcome to the church as we see it today. One of the reasons for the dysfunction is the belief that there is a two-level class structure—a concept of an elite "clergy" (called to the ministry) and the rest as "laity" (the unlearned ones). The reality is, however, that my liver and kidneys are as "called" to serve my body with exactly the same degree of commitment as my head; the *only* difference is one of "*role*." Paul clearly explained this in his letter to the "church" in Corinth, and not just to the clergy, but also to the laity. We have only one head, and that is Jesus. All of us are parts of His body.

But some will say, "Everything has a leader." Maybe so, but leadership is a role to which all of us are called in exactly the same way my liver and kidneys are called to my body; it does not give my head the right to consider my liver and kidneys less important. Every member in my body is subject to the other so that I can exist as a healthy person. In the church setting, we are related to each other through the Holy Spirit. We are subject to Him and each other, irrespective of our roles. Again, Paul

---

190   1 Corinthians 12:27 (TLB).

states: "*Submit to one another out of reverence for Christ.*"[191] It is out of mutual submission and honouring each part of the body that we function as God designed. If the liver and kidneys fail, the waste products of the body will poison us. We are told to give "*honour to whom honour* [is due]"[192] and "*Neither as being lords over God's heritage ...*"[193] If I choose to dishonour my liver and kidneys by not caring for my bodily functions, then within a few days I will die. Welcome to the church of today! We are living on "life support."

The separation of the church into two classes has a second deadly consequence; as "laity," we are not allowed to function in our particular calling, and as the common proverb states, "Use it or you will lose it." We do just that if we are not allowed to engage in our calling. We lose our vision and our purpose, and gradually we die. This creates a mindset that absolves us of our real calling, and instead we become observers, attendees at church, and eventually parasites living off the work of the 20 per cent.

There is a third challenge: if we are deprived of the opportunity to express or develop our calling and decide instead to "do it my way" (to quote Frank Sinatra), then we must heed the warning of Absalom's life and follow the pattern of the relationship between David and King Saul. When one cell decides that it is the centre of the body and requires the body to serve itself, that is called cancer. Both the host and the cancer die at the same time.

For the church to fulfil its mandate from Jesus to "*... go and make disciples of all nations ...*"[194] we need to make sure we are not reproducing the "cancers" of our own life. Instead, we need to replicate the character of our Head, who was not only submitted to the Father but only did and said everything He saw and heard from the Father.

"***All of you together are the one body of Christ*** *...*"[195] (emphasis added). What we are endeavouring to achieve within this local church is just that. If you are prepared to submit to this vision, then we welcome you to take part in changing the eighty-twenty model to the one hundred per cent *body of Christ* pattern as described in scripture.

Shalom.

---

191 Ephesians 5:21 (NIV).

192 Romans 13:7 (KJV).

193 1 Peter 5:3a (KJV).

194 Matthew 28:19 (NIV).

195 1 Corinthians 12:27a (TLB).

35.
HOMEOSTASIS

ACCORDING TO WEBSTER'S NEW WORLD DICTIONARY OF THE AMERICAN *Language*, homeostasis is defined as "balance and equilibrium within an organism." In the medical sense, homeostasis is applied to human life when everything is in complete balance and order—that is, total health for body and soul (though as Christians we would add "spirit" to this equation).

I was struck when I discovered that, medically speaking, there is the expectation of a state of perfect balance, which as we know will never exist because of the DNA of sin. My discovery was also a reminder of the "Eighty-Twenty Principle," which states that in the natural body, all the parts need to be balanced for us to function as God intended.

In the church setting, we are described as the body of Christ, and Paul explains that each of us has a vital and necessary part to play: "... *All of you together are the one body of Christ, and each one of you is a separate and necessary part of it.*"[196] Therefore, in order for the church to enjoy a state of *homeostasis*, we need to be in right relationship with each other. This applies to both our personal attitude and our function within the local church. As the body of Christ, this means making sure we do not say or do anything to attack another member of the body. For example, in the natural body the auto immune system sometimes attacks because it believes that the body is an enemy. However, there is no cure for self destruction.

Cancer is a similar disease. It is the result of our own damaged cells multiplying themselves at the expense of the rest of the body. They gladly use all the services the body supplies, but they are not recognized by the immune system as dangerous because they are of the same family. Only recently has research focused on methods of stimulating the immune system to attack the cancer cells. The parallel between the spiritual and the natural should not escape us. The church often self destructs because it does not maintain or work to create *homeostasis*.

We are told to forgive each other up to seventy times seven and to be generous with mercy and love. Paul describes it as follows:

---

196 1 Corinthians 12:27b (TLB).

Be humble and gentle. Be patient with each other, making allowance for each other's faults because of your love. Try always to be led along together by the Holy Spirit and so be at peace with one another. We are all parts of one body, we have the same Spirit, and we have all been called to the same glorious future.[197]

The second part to *homeostasis* is that each member of the body has to perform the function for which it was designed. We cannot be in balance if one of several parts quit or is prevented from performing the purpose for which it is intended. Therefore, it is not only our personal responsibility but also that of church structure to allow each part to function. On a personal level, it is our duty to discover what "God's calling" is for us, but it is also necessary for the "structure" to recognize and release that calling within the framework of the church. This is the pattern we are endeavouring to follow in this church, so we encourage each one to join us on this wonderful adventure in being a functioning part of the body of Christ.

The third consequence of *homeostasis* is that every action each member makes impacts the whole body to some degree. Part of my brain was recently starved of blood by a stroke, and this impacted *all* the left side of my body. There is nothing that I do in my body that is isolated; every thought, every action has consequence, either good or bad. This is also true for the local church. We *all* feel the results of each other's behaviour, whether we are aware of it or not. Therefore, it behooves us to not focus on self but on Christ, because we are parts of *His body*.

Fourthly, every part of the body is connected to the head, and the flow of instructions comes from the brain. Unless we submit to Jesus as the head of our personal lives, we will never achieve *homeostasis* with Him. Just as in the Trinity in the Godhead, there is a perfect balance of submission, interdependence, headship, and structure … so it follows that we must be in balance within both our personal and church life.

Our actions in the local church impact the church as a whole—first in the region, then the province, then the country, and finally the world! What happens in our corner has consequence for the church universal, whether we like it or not. The theory of quantum physics is based on the principle that the flapping of a butterfly's wings in Brazil can be the first movement of air in an eventual cyclone. Every action, every thought, when added to others, becomes part of change either for good or bad. This same principle can be reflected in the church as we become more like Jesus; God's DNA will connect us more effectively as one body of Christ. This sheds new light on the prayer of Jesus: *"I in them and you in me, all being perfected into*

---

197 Ephesians 4:2–4 (TLB).

*one—**so that the world will know that you sent me and will understand that you love them as much as you love me***"[198] (emphasis added). We will be in *homeostasis* with Jesus and the Father; only then will the world will see Jesus—His church, His body. Jesus said: "*And when I am lifted up on the cross, I will draw everyone to me.*"[199] He also taught us to pray: "*your Kingdom come, your will be done, on earth as it is in heaven.*"[200] Complete *homeostatis*.

Shalom.

198 John 17:23 (TLB).

199 John 12:32 (TLB).

200 Matthew 6:10 (NIV).

36.
NO MORAL COMPASS

*So God created mankind in his own image. He created him in the image of God, he created them **male** and **female**. And God blessed them and said to them "be fruitful and multiply and fill the earth and subdue it and have dominion … "*[201] (emphasis added)

THE WESTERN "CHRISTIANIZED WORLD" HAS PROGRESSIVELY DISMANTLED ITS moral compass and departed from the foundational moral codes that gave rise to its success, instead embracing alternative moral codes or no moral code at all, without realising the personal and social consequences of this. For at least seven thousand years the pattern of marriage has been between a man and a woman. Despite the flawed nature of man, this has remained the foundational relationship of society.

The Bible records some of the consequences of departing from the Creator's design for men and women. Genesis recounts one of these "alternative" lifestyles when two angelic visitors arrive in Sodom to bring "righteous Lot" out of the city because of God's impending judgement; the local men, however, become militant, demanding that Lot surrender his visitors to them: *"… Sodomites, young and old … **surrounded the house and shouted** to Lot, 'Bring out those men so that we can rape them'"*[202] (emphasis added).

I have written articles exposing the intolerance of "militant Islam" as well as "militant Atheism," and now we're seeing "militant sexual perversion"—or to use its politically correct title, "sexual orientation"—rise to the forefront. Case in point, law graduates from a B.C. Christian university are under attack. Even though it's against the Canadian Charter of Rights, businesses are being bullied in an attempt to ban these graduates from practicing law. Moreover, the intolerance degenerates even further as they shift their focus to small Christian businesses. I am personally aware of Christian business people whose businesses have been threatened with closure for not capitulating to their demands.

---

201 Genesis 1:27–28 (ONMB).
202 Genesis 19:4–5 (TLB).

Just as there is no mercy shown by Islam and atheism, it is likewise with the present militant sexual orientation movement. Their strategy is "take no prisoners" until all submit to and accept their lifestyle. We witness the same radical attitude in the Ontario government's mandate to force compliance of both teachers and parents alike with their new sexual teaching program. Furthermore, we are told that there are now seven "sexual orientation options," and New York State is claiming fifty alternatives![203] Consequently, these options have rendered the "male or female" gender choice redundant, and the tragic results are that suicide rates amongst those who claim to be transgender are running at 40 per cent compared with 11.9 per cent amongst heterosexual teens.[204]

In his letter to the church in Rome, the Apostle Paul indicates that even those who have never heard or believed the news of Christ know the truth: "*For the truth about God is known to them instinctively; God has put this knowledge in their hearts.*"[205] When we as a society depart from that understanding, the following happens:

*... so that even their women turned against God's **natural plan** for them and indulged in sex sin with each other. And the men, instead of having **normal** sex relationships with women, burned with lust for each other, men doing shameful things with other men and, as a result, getting paid within their own souls with the penalty they so richly deserved."*[206] (emphasis added)

In rejecting the truth, they suffer the unintended consequences of the depravity of their sin.

Despite the aggressive, militant way in which the sexual orientation agenda is being applied, we as Christians must respond as Jesus would; He loved the sinner without condemning them but warned that their sin would destroy them. For us to behave like Christ requires that we embrace the sinner but not the sin. The Bible states: "*... the love of God is shed abroad in our hearts by the Holy Ghost which is given unto us.*"[207] Any form of retaliation belongs to God, who knows the hearts of all man-

203 Eugene Volokh, "The Volokh Conspiracy," *The Washington Post*, May 17, 2016, https://www.washingtonpost.com/news/volokh-conspiracy/wp/2016/05/17/you-can-be-fined-for-not-calling-people-ze-or-hir-if-thats-the-pronoun-they-demand-that-you-use/?utm_term=.53f57aff4945.

204 Jen Christensen, "LGBQ Teens Face Serious Suicide Risk, Research Finds," *CNN* online, Last modified December 19, 2017, https://www.cnn.com/2017/12/19/health/lgbq-teens-suicide-risk-study/index.html.

205 Romans 1:19 (TLB).

206 Romans 1:26–27 (TLB).

207 Romans 5:5 (KJV).

kind. Many of us have family and friends with sexual lifestyles that do not conform to our biblical beliefs and practices, but our hearts are to love them and pray for them as we would for any other lifestyle or behaviour.

Even though some may mean to harm us, our response must be to pray for them and to send blessing and not cursing; we do have our own course of action. The Apostle Paul tells us that:

> *For we are not fighting against people made of flesh and blood, but against persons without bodies—the evil rulers of the unseen world, those mighty satanic beings and great evil princes of darkness who rule this world; and against huge numbers of wicked spirits in the spirit world. So use every piece of God's armor to resist the enemy whenever he attacks, and when it is all over, you will be left standing up. But to do this, you will need the strong belt of truth and the breastplate of God's approval.*[208]

Behind all the evil in this world lies a satanic kingdom bent on destroying all that is good, and as Paul exhorted, we are to pray and do battle with those "*principalities and powers*"[209] Those displaying militant sexual orientation toward us may not realize it, and would be offended if we suggested it, but to quote Jesus, they are only doing what their father tells them: "*You belong to your father, the devil, and you want to carry out your father's desires. He was a murderer from the beginning, not holding to the truth, for there is no truth in him.*"[210]

Shalom.

---

208   Ephesians 6:12–14 (TLB).

209   Ephesians 6:12 (KJV).

210   John 8:44a (NIV).

37.
WHY DO WE RESIST CHANGE?

"If I could convince you that Christianity was true, would you become a Christian"?

The reply was "no."

This question was posed by a Christian involved in outreach ministry to those who visited his tent at local Ribfests. The answer touches one of the most fundamental issues of life and reveals how reluctant we are to choose change when we are clearly made aware of the need. We do have the power to choose and always retain the ability to say no, whether it relates to lifestyle behaviours, relationships, or, as in this case, our eternal destiny.

As Christians, we deceive ourselves if we think that because we said yes to the original question that we are now different; on truthful examination, we often say no when the need to change stares us in the face. We can be stubborn to the point of our own death, so why is it so difficult to embrace the idea that we should change, and why is change so difficult? Change further challenges us when we do make the necessary decision to persevere enough to get the benefit of that change. Every New Year the gyms are filled with people hoping to lose pounds and become fitter, but those numbers drop dramatically by mid-February.

Parts of the body of Christ believe and embrace the doctrine that we are predestined to salvation, with no ability to choose life unless God has predetermined it. This not only annuls any idea of saying yes or no, but it also appears to contradict the reason for this article. Experience, however, shows that we daily exercise our God-given ability to make choices.

Jesus explained why we refuse to say yes to change when confronted with truth about ourselves: "*This is the judgment ... that men loved the darkness rather than the Light, for their deeds were evil.*"[211] He touches on the real cause of our resistance—we *love* doing and being what we are, despite the consequences. To walk in the fullness of God's plan for us, our transformation requires us to be prepared to change what God says needs to be changed. We need to *love* those things that bring life and want to change those things that bring death. God has granted us the empowerment to

---

211 John 3:19.

change if we are prepared to take that first step of faith. But the question remains: Do we want to change, or do we *love* what we are or do more?

There are further influences at work against us to prevent us from making the changes we need to make. We have an enemy. Satan wants to destroy God's plans for mankind, and he will do all he can by using lies and deceit to frustrate our ability to choose to change. He will use every form of addiction to immobilize our free will and tell us that we cannot change. We are told that Jesus came to *"destroy the works of the devil."*[212] When we engage Jesus in our lives, we have the ability to use divine resources to defeat the devil as well as our own weaknesses so that we can choose to change.

We know that God's ultimate purpose for us is to be changed into the likeness of His Son: *"... to become conformed to the image of His Son ..."*[213] That way God can fully enjoy us and we Him. The process of *change* has to be at the heart of all we do, from our initial conversion experience to when we see Him face to face. In simple terms, Heaven is being in God's presence, and Hell is the opposite.

Moses left this appeal with the children of Israel at the conclusion of his life: *"Look, today I have set before you life and death, depending on whether you obey or disobey."*[214] *"I call heaven and earth to witness against you today I have set before you life and death, blessing or curse. Oh, that you would choose life; and that you and your children might live!"*[215]

How then can we choose life when both our old sinful nature (the influence of this world and the temptation of the devil) are stacked against us? In his letter to the church in Rome, Paul states: *"... cut the nerve of your instinctive actions by obeying the Spirit ..."*[216] We hold the key to change when we take that step of faith to obey the Spirit. He provides the power, the grace, and the enabling to break all the powers that would try to prevent us from choosing life.

Shalom.

---

212 1 John 3:8.

213 Romans 8:29.

214 Deuteronomy 30:15 (TLB).

215 Deuteronomy 30:19 (TLB).

216 Romans 8:13 (PHILLIPS).

38.
HOW TO STEAL FROM YOURSELF

I HAD A FRIEND WHO WAS A SELF-EMPLOYED DESIGNER. ON ONE OCCASION A client told him that his fees were too high, so he agreed to "freelance" on himself by charging a lower rate. He stole from himself. The Old Covenant demanded free will offerings over and above the required 10 per cent of the gross of everything. The "blessings and curses" of Deuteronomy 28 were based on doing to get:

> If you fully obey the Lord your God and carefully follow all his commands ... the Lord your God will set you high above all the nations on earth. All these blessings will come upon you... However, if you do not obey the Lord your God and do not carefully follow all his commands and decrees I am giving you today, all these curses will come on you and overtake you."[217]

Malachi reinforces this position; "Will a mere mortal rob God? Yet you rob me. But you ask, 'How are we robbing you?' In tithes and offerings. You are under a curse ..."[218] To drive it even deeper, God undergirds the agreement He has with Israel by reminding them of the consequences of disobedience: "All these curses will come on you. They will pursue you and overtake you until you are destroyed ..."[219] "Their failure to keep their part of the agreement concerning tithes resulted in Israel experiencing a famine, but according to the contract, God offered a solution to the curse:

> Bring all the tithes into the storehouse so that there will be food enough in my Temple; if you do, I will open the windows of heaven for you and pour out a blessing so great you won't have room to take it in!"[220]

But Israel's obedience did not depend on their heart being right any more than my heart is rejoicing when I pay Revenue Canada. They demand ... I pay. End of

---

217   Deuteronomy 28:1–2, 15 (NIV).
218   Malachi 3:8–9 (NIV).
219   Deuteronomy 28:45a (NIV).
220   Malachi 3:10 (TLB).

story. But the Kingdom of God as revealed fully by Jesus goes for the real issue: What is the attitude of my heart? Israel came to this point by default. God's intent was a personal relationship with His people, but you only have to read the story of Jacob to realize that man's relationship with God was based on works. (If I do this, will you do that?). But those are the terms of the old contract.

Jesus' fulfillment of the law took righteousness to the next level in that God considers a man guilty of adultery for just looking at a woman lustfully. In the case of giving, you *do not let your left hand know what your right hand is doing.*[221] In today's society, this includes those imposing false guilt on people when appealing for gifts for "the ministry." ("Who will give a thousand dollars? Yes, I see that hand.")

Jesus states: "... *for of the abundance of the heart his mouth speaketh.*"[222] God is after a pure heart, but that requires a new and better covenant based on the principle of God giving everything. The expression of that principle is in the total sacrifice of God's only begotten Son so that we can enter "the Holy of Holies" in order to have the intimacy with God He desires.

The old hymn states: "Nothing in my hands I bring, simply to the cross I cling."[223] I can do nothing to receive mercy and grace, healing, deliverance, or blessing—financial or otherwise— by keeping any legal agreement. It is all about God's attitude of *grace* toward us. It's free for us, but it cost God everything. How does grace work? I avail myself of this incredible gift simply by admitting my sin, repenting of it, then receiving His forgiveness by faith. I can only do that because of all that Jesus has done.

There is much more than I have listed here, but the principle is that even though we didn't care or bother with Him, our Divine Lover gave Himself totally for our sakes; "*This is love: not that we loved God, but that he loved us and sent his Son as an atoning sacrifice for our sins.*"[224] In the light of such generosity, our only true response has to be, "I, in return, give You my wretched life, my failures, problems, financial mess, broken body, and everything else that's damaged." Now that's a deal any one in their right mind should not refuse!

So how do we steal from ourselves? Given God's kindness in all He has done, how can we rob ourselves of a giving attitude by being so stingy and withholding what He has given us? God gave "the works, 100 per cent." This relationship, like a marriage, only works well when both give "the works." That's everything. If you want

---

221 Matthew 6:3 (NIV)

222 Luke 6:45b (KJV).

223 August Toplady, "Rock of Ages," 1763.

224 1 John 4:10 (NIV).

an indicator of the degree of this "giving the works" in your own life, consider how much you're giving financially. God says that we cannot serve both God and money.[225] When describing God's commitment to us, the hymn "When I Survey" says that such love shall have my soul, my life, my all. A contemporary translation inserts the word "demands" instead of "shall have," but according to the New Agreement, I get to choose to give Him my all. If I don't, then I'm the one who loses.

I steal from myself when I fail to "surrender all to Jesus." At one point in my Christian life I remember someone teaching me to give the tithe based on the "gross," which I did faithfully as part of "the law" understanding at that time. Then I heard that it could be based on the "net," and I reduced my giving! It revealed that my heart was under law, not grace. The actual consequence was that we experienced fourteen lean years. So what did that prove? Was it that the law as stated in Malachi was correct, or did it expose what was in my heart? Perhaps a little of both. As soon as my heart turned to the law, I was under the curse of the law, but as I repented and turned to grace, my inheritance was the blessing of God.

There are principles and there are laws. The basis of the laws are sound principles, but they do not get at the heart's motives; only the Holy Spirit and scripture can expose what's hidden in my heart. Sadly, *I stole from myself* because my heart attitude *was wrong* in my giving. According to the New Agreement, I own nothing. I acknowledge that God loves me, and if my heart is right, then I want please the One who loves with such total commitment.

Shalom.

---

225 Luke 16:13

39.
THE FATHER, OUR FATHER, AND MY FATHER

DURING MY WIFE BRENDA'S LEADING OF THE COMMUNION RECENTLY, SHE LISTED a number of names and adjectives describing the character and the person of both God and Christ. These words helped build a clear picture of God Himself that is, to some degree, trying to know the unknowable. Orthodox Judaism will not even write His name let alone speak it because of the reverence and holiness that they feel surrounds the revelation of God.

In Matthew 6:9 Jesus shares a prayer with His disciples, and in various biblical translations, we hear about the honour due God's name: *"hallowed be your name"* (NIV), *"Your name must at once be made holy"* (ONMB), *"We honor your holy name,"* (TLB), *"May your name be honoured"* (PHILLIPS). In the light of such awe, God has reached out to His creation by revealing Himself in one of the most personal of *all* relationships—our Father. This revelation of the role and character of God is so important that Jesus revealed Him as the first and ultimate Father when He said: *"And you should not call anyone on earth your father, for One is your heavenly father."*[226] He is the true model of the word *father*, just as Jesus is the perfect model of the *son*.

This is wonderful news for us, because it establishes not only His role, but also the person of God, how He relates to us, and how we are to relate to Him. David understood this when he wrote: *"Like as a father pitieth his children, so the Lord pitieth them that fear him. For he knoweth our frame; he remembereth that we are dust."*[227] We can take great encouragement from this word picture, especially when we feel we have failed and sinned so badly, even like the prodigal son or the self-righteous brother.

Jesus talks about Him as the author of all life, both physical and spiritual: *"The Father has life in himself, and has granted his Son to have life in himself ..."*[228] (emphasis added). Even in the final judgement, Jesus ascribes his submission to Him: *"But I pass no judgement without consulting the Father"*[229] (emphasis added). He is the

---

226   Matthew 23:9 (OMB).

227   Psalm 103:13–14 (KJV).

228   John 5:26 (TLB).

229   John 5:30a (TLB).

eternal *Father, the true Father of everything*. In this sense, He is the *Father* of all living saved and unsaved, even though by unbelief we make Satan our father.

To confirm his role as Messiah, Jesus makes this statement: "*I refer to the miracles I do; these have been assigned to me by **the Father** and they prove that **the Father** has sent me*"[230] (emphasis added). To endorse His Sonship, Jesus states to His disciples: "*I am the way—yes, and the Truth and the Life. No one can get to **the Father** except by means of me*"[231] (emphasis added). He also explains that "*... to welcome me is to welcome **the Father** who sent me*"[232] (emphasis added).

Of course, we will sometimes be plagued by disbelief, as was Philip: "*... Sir, show us **the Father** and we will be satisfied*"[233] (emphasis added). Jesus replies: "*Anyone who has seen me has seen **the Father***"[234] (emphasis added). Paul tells us that Jesus is "*the image of the invisible God,*"[235] and the writer to the Hebrews states: "*This **Son**, radiance of the glory of God, flawless expression of the nature of God ...*"[236] (emphasis added). These verses answer Philip's question. Jesus shows us fully what *the Father* is like. Look no further than Jesus and interpret the Old Covenant and scriptures through the words of Jesus. This will help avoid issues related to following Old Covenant rules and processes. *Jesus at the centre of it all.*

It's thrilling that Jesus also reveals that God is *our Father* and makes the relationship both personal and collective. When He tells us to pray to *our Father* in heaven, He's saying that God is not just *the Father* but *our Father*. When we do that, we are recognizing that as believers we have *one* common *Father* and that makes us family, all brothers and sisters. Although this is commonly known within the church universal, it should also be our practice. Having stated that point, I am reminded that siblings do not always agree and act like family; therefore, sometimes our Father has to crack a few heads if we are to be united so that we can become the spotless bride for his Son.

Some feel we might be disrespectful by addressing God as our "friend," but God now calls us his *sons* and loves us as much as he loves *the Son*. You don't get more intimate than that, except perhaps when we become the *bride* of Christ. Jesus makes it very clear that God is *His Father*, and He confirms that He is the Messiah

---

230   John 5:36 (TLB).
231   John 14:6 (TLB).
232   John 13:20b (TLB).
233   John 14:8 (TLB).
234   John 14:9b (TLB).
235   Colossians 1:15 (NIV).
236   Hebrews 1:3b (PHILLIPS).

through the miracles He does, which are not done in His own name: *"The proof is in the miracles I do in the name of **my Father**"*[237] (emphasis added). He further states that belief in Him as the *Son* brings eternal life: *"For it is **my Father's** will that everyone who sees his **Son** and believes on him should have eternal life—that I should raise him at the Last Day"*[238] (emphasis added).

The Jewish leaders were ready to stone Jesus to death when He uttered the words, *"I and **the Father are one**"*[239] (emphasis added), because this made him equal with God. But the plans of the Father become even more exciting when Jesus prays for those who will believe in him:

> *I do not ask concerning them only, but also concerning those who believe in me because of the disciples message, so that **all would be one, just as you Father are in me and i in you,** that they also would be in **us**, so that the world would believe that you sent me."*[240] (emphasis added)

The evidence that Jesus has come is revealed in His church by the *unity* between the *Son*, the *Father*, and *each other*, which is the expression of love for one another. You cannot have unity without love. This relationship is confirmed by the Holy Spirit with the evidence of signs and miracles following the preaching of the Word.

Welcome to the real church. Will you join us on the journey with this goal? Shalom.

---

237 John 10:25 (TLB).
238 John 6:40 (TLB).
239 John 10:30 (TLB).
240 John 17:20–21 (OMB).

40.
DISRESPECT

ONE OF THE ADVANTAGES OF AGE IS THAT YOU GET TO LOOK BACK AND compare things from the past with the present. Even though our understanding can often be coloured by nostalgia, I think I see very clearly on the issue of disrespect. As a child, I recall that there was an expected respect for those in authority, such as school teachers, policemen, neighbours, relatives, adults—all people older than you, particularly parents. Not that these authority figures were always right or even good, but there existed a principle of "*honour to whom honour* [is due]."[241] While this attitude was birthed out of Christianity, it permeated society at large.

All authority originates from God, but because society has become increasingly more secular, it has dispensed with God and Christianity as its moral code. Consequently, civilization has exposed itself to blatant, self-centred behaviour patterns that show no respect for anything or anyone except self. Self is the god of the age in Western society, and because of the breakdown of authority and the chain of respect, the rebellious attitudes of others continuously challenge those exercising authority.

My personal testimony, even as a Christian, was that I thought my boss was incompetent. I may have been right, but I destroyed him behind his back with words of disrespect and criticism. As I moved from job to job and continent to continent (Europe to Africa, back to the U.K., and then to Canada), the bosses got progressively worse and even more incompetent than the previous one. It was probably my practice of criticism that honed my view of the level of ineptitude in my bosses.

This journey took me through fourteen years of personal agony until one day the "penny dropped" (old English expression for access to a public toilet). I needed to learn to submit to authority, even to those who were incompetent, poor, weak, lazy, or any other inadequacy they may have had. I didn't have to agree with them, but my attitude needed to change to one of honouring and respecting.

Ultimately, all authority begins and ends with God. If we don't honour those in authority, then we are actually rebelling against God. We will not only pay the consequences in the here and now, but we will answer for it when we stand before Him on judgement day. In his classic book *The Tale of Three Kings*, Gene Edwards

---

241   Romans 13:7 (KJV).

tells the story of David and his submission to Saul. Even though Saul abused his authority and planned to kill him, it was David's attitude of honouring God's anointed ruler that prevented him from taking Saul's life, even when he had the opportunity to do so. This attitude was also seen when David's son, Absalom, plotted a rebellion against God's anointed king, David, in order to remove him from the throne. The story clearly exposes the heart of each man, and both Saul and Absalom came to an unhappy end.

The commandment says this: *"Honour your father and your mother, so that you may live long in the land the Lord your God is giving you."*[242] My Father died two years before my conversion experience when I was sixteen. He was not a perfect father, but even at my present age I must still honour my parents, even though they are deceased. How dramatically our attitude and understanding changes toward our mom and dad when we ourselves become parents.

Now we get to "meddling."

Honour Christ by submitting to each other. You wives you must submit to your husbands' leadership in the same way you submit to the Lord ... And you husbands, show the same kind of love to your wives as Christ showed to the Church when he died for her.[243]

I'm not sure which of these two instructions is the most difficult to obey; it's probably the one that applies to us!

Of course, there are always objections. It's easy to spot imperfections in others but we always judge from our strengths and are usually blind to our own shortcomings. I have shared some of mine, but we need to honour Christ by submitting to each other, because the way we treat one another is the way we treat Christ. At Saul's dramatic road to Damascus conversion, Jesus clearly states that he'd been persecuting Him each time he killed or imprisoned believers: "Saul, Saul, why do you persecute me?"[244]

"But," you might say, "you don't know my spouse." Well, maybe not, but God does, and He says *"My grace is sufficient for you, for my power is made perfect in weakness."*[245] God commands us to follow the scriptural pattern He has laid out for us; you don't have to agree, nor do you have to be a door mat, but you do need to remember

---

242 Exodus 20:12 (NIV).
243 Ephesians 5:21–22, 25 (TLB).
244 Acts 9:4 (NIV).
245 2 Corinthians 12:9a (NIV).

that the one to whom you submit is ultimately responsible to God. Like David, you can remove yourself from abusive authority. David had two opportunities to kill Saul, but because his heart was right, God vindicated him. *"Vengeance is mine; I will repay,"*[246] says God. True vindication will come at the judgement, but as much as is in me, I want to get this right before that day.

All true authority comes from God, and with it comes accountability according to the degree of responsibility. *"All of you together are the one body of Christ, and each one of you is a separate and **necessary** part of it"*[247] (emphasis added). One of my tasks is not only to encourage everyone to function in the roles to which God has called them, but as much as possible also facilitate opportunity to grow in it. Let us therefore "give honour to whom honour is due."

Shalom.

---

246 Romans 12:19b (KJV).
247 1 Corinthians 12:27 (TLB).

41.
YOUR FATHER

WE HAVE LOOKED IN THE LATEST ARTICLE AT THE PROGRESSION FROM *THE Father* to *our Father* and the ultimate *my Father* relationship with God, but there is also a danger of regression to *your Father*. The Jews claimed that they were the children of Abraham by birth, but Jesus addresses the teachers of the law with these words: *"For you are the children of your father the devil and you love to do the evil things he does. He was a murderer from the beginning and a hater of truth..."*[248] He is not speaking about their earthly parents, but their *spiritual father*, whom they revealed by their behaviour.

This is about as radical a statement as you can get, because it divides men into two camps. The Jewish interpretation of the Law of Moses produced both a belief and practice that Jesus saw as an expression of Satan, not God. They said: *"... Aren't we right in saying that you are a Samaritan and demon-possessed?"*[249] How can this be? They memorized huge portions of scripture and obeyed the 613 laws as well as their man-made traditions, so how could they possibly be children of the devil?

The Apostle Paul provides an explanation: *"The law never succeeded in producing righteousness—the failure was always the weakness of human nature ..."*[250] Self righteous works only produce pride. Pride was the first sin, and Satan the first sinner. Just like the rest of God's creation, he reproduces after his own kind. All efforts of Christians (or variations of Christianity), Muslims, or any other religion that relies on self achievement, however noble in appearance, is simply a reflection of their father, the devil.

Yes, all the nice, good people, works of charity, self sacrifice, and so on from the highest positions in government, churches, or nations belong to the devil. We easily accept the lives of evil dictators as the fruit of Satan, but how do we classify nice Christians and people who run international charities? The good are always the biggest enemy of the best.

---

248 John 8:44a (TLB).
249 John 8:48 (NIV).
250 Romans 8:3 (PHILLIPS).

So what's the problem? The root issue is *self*. We have made even the nice self, the kind, loving self, central, and in doing so we have replaced God as the centre of our universe. That's exactly what Satan did, and the Bible tells us that he can appear as an "angel of light." The real motive of the heart is revealed when the "nice people" are challenged. Jesus' confrontation with the religious of His day caused them to be so insulted that it exposed the murder that was already deeply embedded in their hearts. We say we are kind and caring, but when our true motive is exposed, we join the crowd and cry "Crucify! Crucify!"

This is the reason that the first "beautiful attitude" in Matthew's Gospel is humility. Humility enables me to see myself in the light of God so that I quickly admit that I am a sinner in need of forgiveness and the grace to become the *Father's son*—at least for a little while. Then I find that feeling rising up in me that I am not such a bad person after all—look how I tithe, read the scriptures, attend meetings, worship, and pray. All of these are vital disciplines, but my heart can turn the most beautiful of experiences into reflections of my previous father by pride. I am torn between two camps—one of self righteousness and one of utter despair and failure. I often oscillate between the two opposite poles. Paul said that it is "*Not by works of righteousness that we have done, but by his mercy he saved us ...*"[251] This keeps us from the consuming danger of pride.

I need to be aware that I am on a journey toward a destiny that completes itself with God. Life can be cruel, unkind, and unforgiving, but as we keep our hearts humble before Him, He gives us the grace to continue to the end. God Himself is the final destination: *The Father, Our Father, and My Father.*

Shalom.

---

251 Titus 3:5 (KJV).

42.
REAL MOTIVES

Because we are in the middle of a federal election, I have observed how the political parties jostle for the hearts and minds of voters with promises that they will, if elected, have difficulty fulfilling. The motivation for these promises to spend our money can be called "political convenience," and it makes us question their real motives. They are not always based on sound moral or practical beliefs, but rather simply appeal to the voters in order to gain support.

We live in countries that still suffer from decisions made from motives of "political convenience." Every act of political convenience will produce its own children, and those who choose not to study history are bound to repeat the same mistakes. The war in Iraq and its consequences (orchestrated by deceit) continues to torment the world.

Eve's seduction by the serpent was based on the idea that eating from the tree of the knowledge of good and evil would make her be like God. Choosing the short-cut to achieve God's purpose of man becoming like Him, instead of eating from the tree of "life," seemed a good idea at the time. We all suffer the consequences of that act of flawed motive for "political convenience."

Sarah's suggestion that Abraham take her slave girl to provide an heir as a means of achieving God's promise seemed very convenient. Sarah was old and barren, and technically the child born to Hagar was her property … problem solved! But history tells a different story. We clearly see the fruit of Sarah's decision in the Middle East today; there is no hope of reconciling the Israelis and Arabs.

Islam traces its roots back to Abraham and Hagar. As a consequence of Sarah's plan, the children of Hagar hate the children of Sarah and are determined to exterminate them. God's promise was that all the nations of the earth would be blessed by the children of Abraham, but the children of Hagar are determined to force the entire world to submit ("Islam" means to submit by any method) to Allah.

High Priest Caiaphas made a decision of political convenience relative to Jesus when he stated: *"You stupid idiots – let this man die for the people—why should the whole nation perish?"*[252] Under the Roman system, they had security and authority,

---

252 John 11:49b–50 (TLB).

and they saw Jesus jeopardizing their position and status. His motives were faulty. Some forty years later the Roman general Titus destroyed Jerusalem, scattering the Jews around the world and leaving them without a homeland for nineteen hundred years until it was restored in 1948.

Pilate trapped himself into making a faulty motive decision because he had taken bribes from Caiaphas in appointing him High Priest. Despite his knowledge of Christ's innocence, his bribery left him with no alternative but to respond to the cries of "Crucify! Crucify!"

Political decisions of convenience have both short and long-term pain, and when applied to our personal lives, the consequences are the same. When we make changes to our understanding of God's Word to suit family or personal moral issues for convenience sake, we can expect both short and long term negative results. Understanding deeper truths is one thing, but changing the fundamentals of the faith is another. Being a "Pentecostal" doesn't have much social status, and being classified as a "fundamentalist" even less so, but do we change our name and affiliation for political convenience?

In the nineteenth century the church was assaulted with liberal theology that denied the virgin birth, resurrection, miracles, and divine inspiration of the Bible. For most mainline denominations, it was politically convenient to embrace these errors for fear of looking less than intelligent … a flawed motive. The fruit of that motive is the closing of church doors and dwindling congregations.

Secular society looks at the church as an outdated organization based on superstition. Consequently, the teaching of creation and moral biblical principles in schools is now prohibited. We have a society that has legalized every form of sexual perversion. Let us set ourselves to live lives of truth, with no decisions of convenience in faith, doctrine, or practice—whatever the outcome—because history tells us that vindication is coming to God's people. David records: *"Who shall ascend into the hill of the Lord? or who shall stand in his holy place? He that has clean hands, and a **pure heart** …"*[253] (emphasis added). Our real motives have to be pure for everything we do.

Whether we are small, insignificant, mocked, or laughed at by those who consider themselves the elite of this world, our cry must be that of Joshua: *"… as for me and my household, we will serve the Lord."*[254] Let us rather be fools for Christ.

Shalom.

---

253   Psalm 24:3–4a (KJV).
254   Joshua 24:15 (NIV).

43.
THE WORD BECAME FLESH

As a congregation, we have focused on a "move of God" for the last two years but were not sure how this would manifest. We studied the Welsh Revival and prayed for a divine visitation that would make our lives more like Christ so that we could fulfil the commission of reaching the lost. We studied Rick Joyner's book, *The Call*, in order to develop the vision of total commitment to God's plans and purposes. But what would be the signs and evidence that our prayers are being answered?

Some of us have participated in the "moves of God" over the years and are aware that we are looking for something greater, deeper, and more permanent than what we had experienced in the past. The initial danger would be to expect a repeat of historical events or our own experiences, so let us look at some of the things that are happening almost "under the radar."

We've had numerous prophetic words indicating that what we'll be moving into will be different than the past, and because we weren't given the specifics, we will have to continue pursuing God in order to find His purpose. I have been struck by several situations that are different from any others in my personal experience, such as the number of people attending the prayer meetings. We are currently running with 30 per cent of those attending the congregation, and many of them have never been part of this type of meeting before.

Secondly, the participation of those who prayed was 100 per cent this last Tuesday. There is a passion and desire for public prayer; sometimes we gather around each other to pray and lay hands on one another while others we anoint with oil. We are enjoying the freedom in sharing testimony of both our successes and failures as the love we have for each other spills over into our fellowship times. We are experiencing the manifest presence of God in all our gatherings, and the awareness is increasing, particularly in the Sunday worship time. The prophetic is being released in a more sensitive way. There is a demonstration of "body ministry" among more of the congregation. As a result, we are discovering teaching and preaching giftings amongst us that are encouraging and edifying us all.

Those who already have a teaching gift are speaking above and beyond their usual level. From my own experience, I am at a loss to explain why I can prepare for hours pages of typed notes and scripture references only to find that when I come to deliver the "Word," it pours out of me like water without specific reference to the structure of my notes. This has happened so many times that I must attribute it to God's manifest presence in our gatherings. By saying this, I don't mean to ignore the study and process of teaching that has been my style; it's the new that complements the old, not replaces it.

I was meditating on these issues before God in prayer and this is what came to me: As I looked up, my heart and mind were open, and I experienced an awareness of God's presence beyond anything I had previously encountered. It then occurred to me that I've been in this place regularly in recent months; I have been entering a greater consciousness of God. The word I sensed from God was "The word was becoming flesh in me." I was becoming the Word of God in the flesh. At first, I recoiled from the thoughts, because I was immediately aware that I was only a sinner saved by grace—heresy! I wondered if it was pride. But then a peace flooded my thoughts as I recognized the work of the Spirit. I was unaware that Christ was being formed in me (Galatians 4:19) to a greater degree, and that these manifestations and anointings were the evidence of that work.

The wonderful process of being conformed to the image of Christ is happening to us all, and because we are starting to make Jesus the centre of our lives, the centre of His church, we hardly notice that work being done. His Holy Spirit has been operating in us "under the radar."

What then is our future? Just as this process has been partially hidden to us, so I believe we are to trust Him for each step and continue to be Christ-centric in all that we do. We should not change direction until we have the assurance from the Spirit of God: *"Your ears will hear a word behind you, 'This is the way, walk in it, whenever you turn to the right or to the left.'"*[255]

All past "revivals" have had a divine impact that has lasted for a period of time. The Welsh Revival lasted ten months, although the effects are still with us today. But I sense that God is working more progressively until the Word becomes flesh in us (John 1:14). Just as Jesus was both the Word of God and the expression of God in the flesh, so we will be the image and expression of Jesus to the lost. Whether there will be a moment in time, another Pentecost, we do not know … but the way to make the encounters with God permanent is to be changed, conformed to the image of Christ. We are becoming a bride for his Son, *"… having no spot or wrinkle or any such thing …"*[256]

---

255   Isaiah 30:21.
256   Ephesians 5:27.

"Teach me thy way, O Lord, and lead me in a plain path …"[257]
Shalom.

44.
WHO OR WHAT ARE YOU LIVING FOR?

SOMEONE RECENTLY SHARED THE THOUGHT THAT THEIR ONLY REASON FOR living was their children. Although this may have been an oversimplification of their life's purpose, it was their prime focus and motivation. We could be critical of them having such a limited vision, but on the positive side, they came to the point of recognizing they had an actual reason for living. The goal was a wholesome one— "other centred" and outside their personal benefit.

There are a multitude of "things" people live for that are self-centred. I heard the obituary of a man who lived a wasted life in petty crime who said that "all he ever wanted was a Cadillac." General Motors was the only beneficiary of his life! But what happens to our motivation for living if that reason is removed? What if our children die, or we never get to own the Cadillac? We can add to that any other purpose or passion. We can quickly spin out of control into a self-destructive death spiral of bitterness. There is the mother who loses her son and then spends the rest of her life mourning him and blaming God; and then there are the First Nations people who are suffering an epidemic of suicide, especially amongst their youth. Our secular society has removed God from the curriculum of life, and there is no hope. Without Him all we have is this short span of existence in which we hope death takes away the pain.

As Christians, we "… *do not grieve like the rest of mankind, who have no hope.*"[258] We have a final destiny with God, all because of what Jesus has done. But do we have a reason or vision for living in the *now*, or are we just "marking time" until Jesus comes? One of the weaknesses of the teaching of the rapture of the church has been a form of spiritual suicide. Paul addresses this clearly in his second letter to the church in Thessalonica. Paul, when under pressure and extreme persecution, faced the same challenge when he declared that he was torn between the desire to depart to be with Christ (which he considered far better) or remain on earth for the sake of the welfare of the church.

---

258   1 Thessalonians 4:13b (NIV).

We therefore need to examine the real reasons for living. In his letter to the Thessalonians, Paul urges them not to aim to please men, but to please God.[259] Because his goal was God first and not self, he was able serve others without serving becoming the reason for living. The scripture does state that, *"Where there is no vision, the people perish ..."*[260] This statement not only conveys the hope that a vision or purpose gives us, but also that the consequences of failure have purpose. Without vision we have no hope; without hope we atrophy until we shrink and die both physically and spiritually.

As in the case of the prodigal son; *"When he came to his senses, he said ... I will ..."*[261] He had to come to the end of himself before he could take action to rebuild his life. It is never, never, never too late. One of the crucified thieves next to Jesus at the point of death found a moment of life while the other missed the Saviour of the world. As Moses exhorted—choose life!

God has an ultimate, glorious purpose for each of us, way beyond our wildest dreams or understanding. While we are on earth, each and every day is part of that destiny. May God give us grace to walk in faith until we know as we are known: *"... then shall I know fully, even as I am fully known."*[262]

We pray, *"your kingdom come, your will be done, on earth even as it is in heaven."*[263] I confess that in the past I had projected that prayer only into future fulfilment, but I have since applied it to the present. Your kingdom come *now* in me; Your will be done *now* in me, just as it is in heaven. I am reminded that every angel, cherubim, or heavenly host does His will continually, and Jesus said that the Son can do nothing by himself; he can only do what he sees the Father doing (John 5:19). That has become my prayer.

My vision is to see that prayer come into greater reality to the degree that it is possible this side of heaven, and that it starts with myself, then this local church, then finally *"make disciples of all nations ..."*[264]

But thanks be to God! He gives us the victory through our Lord Jesus Christ.
Therefore, my dear brothers and sisters, stand firm. Let nothing move you.

---

259   1 Thessalonians 2:4.

260   Proverbs 29:18a (KJV).

261   Luke 15:17a, 18a (NIV).

262   1 Corinthians 13:12b (NIV).

263   Matthew 6:10 (NIV).

264   Matthew 28:19 (NIV).

*Always give yourselves **fully** to the work of the Lord, because you know that your labor in the Lord is not in vain.*[265] (emphasis added)

Shalom.

---

265   1 Corinthians 15:57–58 (NIV).

45.
THE SILENT KILLER

CANCER IS CALLED THE "SILENT KILLER" BECAUSE IT GROWS AND METASTASIZES in our bodies before any signs or physical evidence can be seen or experienced. Because the cancer is a corruption of our own cells, it circumvents the immune system, deceiving it into believing it is friendly and part of the family.

Life appears normal until suddenly the hidden damage is revealed and we face the destructive evidence in our own bodies. Present cures require killing both cancerous and good cells in the hope that the body can survive the invasion and recover. The latest experimental cures include methods of alerting the immune system to recognize these wayward cells and destroy them.

A parallel exists between cancer and sin in the life of the Christian. Sin manifests itself as a "silent killer" within the person, which will eventually infect first the local church then the church universal. Just as cancer first impacts one part of the body (the individual believer), it then proceeds to metastasize to the rest of the body. Whatever we do, whether good or bad, secretly or openly, will impact the spiritual health of the church. We may not be aware of its existence for a time, but just like cancer, it will reap its deadly consequences. Likewise, the private devotion of our secret lives will bring life to the whole body. None of us are an island unto ourselves, and we bring either blessings or curses to the whole church.

There are things we can do to help our own immune system, one of which is to eat "live food" such as vegetables, fruit, and nuts because they contain antioxidants that support our defence system and attack rogue cells Similarly, our spiritual life can be built up with "live food" from God through the Bible, prayer, and worship. We need to do this individually as well as corporately. Over-cooked vegetables and processed food will do more damage; therefore, to remain healthy we must individually develop an appetite for "live food" from God.

In my article entitled "The Word Became Flesh," the premise is that God's purpose for us is to become like his Son. The "silent killer" is aimed at frustrating that divine plan, and Satan will do all he can and use any method to do that, especially by employing subtle religious devices. When we studied the Welsh Revival of 1904, it was clear that the devil used a devout Christian, Jesse Penn Lewis, to convince Evan Roberts that he was in danger of taking glory that belonged to God. She encouraged him to withdraw from the revival, which he did. He never spoke publicly again, and the outward manifestation of that revival died. He himself died a recluse in 1951.

Just as the latest attempts to defeat cancer look to alerting our own immune system, so our spiritual immune system is complemented by God's Holy Spirit as He convicts of sin then provides "... *grace to help us in our time of need.*"[266] The cancer of sin has its own ally in Satan, who will use his lies and deception to defuse the work of the Spirit. Paul recognizes his methods and states: "*We don't want Satan to win any victory here, and well we know his methods.*"[267] God promises: "*For he rescues you from every trap ...*"[268] The KJV says it this way: "*snare of the fowler.*"

As with cancer, we can't deal with it on our own. The truth is, we are all cancer patients of sin, and it will manifest its addictive nature in us to varying degrees. But God has a treatment and cure for sin. Only He can deliver us from the present and ultimate consequences of this cancer. We have a deliverer for both the cause and cure of this cancer in Jesus Christ, who "*Because he himself suffered when he was tempted, he is able to help those who are being tempted.*"[269] Scripture tells us:

> For we do not have a high priest who is unable to empathize with our weaknesses, but we have one who has been tempted in every way, just as we are— yet he did not sin. Let us then approach God's throne of grace with confidence, so that we may receive mercy and find grace to help in our time of need.[270]

There are aggressive forms of cancer that attack with such force that we appear to have only days to live. The same applies to our spiritual lives, but we have this confidence from God that, "*When the enemy shall come in like a flood, the Spirit of the Lord will raise up a standard against him.*"[271] God's grace is at our disposal through the work of the Holy Spirit. Paul states: "*Here is my advice. Live your whole life in the Spirit* [continually be being filled] *and you will not satisfy the desires of the lower nature.*"[272]

Cancer support groups help those during the fight, and God has also set us in families of believers to stand with us. Sometimes the DNA of sin overcomes us and

---

266   Hebrews 4:16b (NIV).

267   2 Corinthians 2:11b (PHILLIPS).

268   Psalm 91:3a (TLB).

269   Hebrews 2:18 (NIV).

270   Hebrews 4:15–16 (NIV).

271   Isaiah 59:19b (KJV).

272   Galatians 5:16 (PHILLIPS).

we fall to the "silent killer," but we can find forgiveness and restoration. Paul also tells us:

> *Dear brothers, if a Christian is overcome by some sin, you who are godly should gently and humbly help him back on the right path, remembering that next time it might be one of you who is in the wrong."*[273]

We are not to shoot our wounded.

God is the ultimate realist and has made full provision for dealing with the cancer of sin. His final goal is to turn us into "The Word Becoming Flesh" so that we who are sinners by nature are given a new one when we become sons of God by rebirth. It is only then that Holy Spirit enables new behaviour and character so that collectively as a congregation we become "The Word Made Flesh."

Shalom.

---

273   Galatians 6:1 (TLB).

46.
THE FLOODGATES OF HEAVEN

As a church, we have been praying and preparing for what we call "a move of God." Part of the preparation was the study of the Welsh Revival based on the book *The World Aflame* by Rick Joyner. In addition to our desire to see an awakening in the church, we also wanted to learn the lessons from that divine visitation so that we would know what to embrace and what to avoid.

Not only was it important to explore the actual happenings but also the history that birthed the revival. It was at least a thirty-year process in which the hunger grew amongst a few with the vision for change. We share, I believe, a similar pattern and desire. At this point it does not require the thousands but the committed few, and I believe we are the committed few "... *for such a time as this*."[274]

One of the tragedies of the Welsh Revival was that it was so short in its initial outpouring (almost like a thunderstorm from heaven) and it was only ten months before God's vehicle, Evan Roberts, was seduced into believing that he was in danger of stealing God's glory. Despite the brevity, there are still many signs still with us; for example, when we "sing with our spirits" (1 Corinthians 14:15), as this occurred for the first time in recent history in Wales.

Every act of divine intervention involves a human partner and is always a balance between the sovereignty of God and man's free will. We must avoid elevating the person, but we should honour the vessel God chooses to use. Those who demand that an awakening must be all of God will never enter a divine visitation and only criticize those who do.

During the Welsh Revival, it was as though the floodgates of heaven opened, but much was lost because of lack of preparation. When a thunderstorm breaks, the ground can only absorb as much water as it is *open* to receive. Soil that has not been plowed allows the majority of rain to be lost, but my "prophetic ear" senses that God is breaking up our topsoil of apathy and indifference and is stirring us with a passion and desire for the sweet rain from heaven. We are becoming an assembly of hungry people for God's presence and agenda.

---

274 Esther 4:14b (NIV).

God has shown us "extreme" mercy as a mature congregation of seasoned saints and continues to work the soil of our hearts so that we are ready to receive the floodgates from heaven. The results we are praying for will be a fruitful crop, some thirty, some fifty, and some even a hundred per cent for the perfecting of the church and the salvation of the world. We are looking that our families, friends, neighbours, communities, local churches, province, our land, and even to "*the uttermost part of the earth*"[275] be impacted ... no small dream.

A vital part of the preparation is the deepening of our intimacy with God in prayer and worship. I have been challenged to pray daily, "Your Kingdom come *now in me*, Your will be done *now in me*, just like it is in heaven (Matthew 6:10). Attendance at our prayer meeting continues to increase, and my heart cries out, "*teach us to pray.*"[276]

In the article "The Word Became Flesh," I outlined some of the things God has been working on in me. On Sunday, six people added their experience, and others will be adding their testimony in the coming days. These experiences are creating canals and riverbeds for the outpouring of God's floodgates from heaven. We don't want landslides, or water running off dry ground, but God's presence directed to His perfect will and agenda. We don't want to have history look back and see how it was like the Welsh Revival that only lasted ten months.

We are on tiptoe waiting for the promise of:

*I will repay for the years the locusts have eaten ... And afterward, I will pour out my Spirit on **all** people. Your sons and daughters will prophesy, your old men will dream dreams, your young men will see visions. Even on my servants, both men and women, I will pour out my Spirit in those days.*"[277] (emphasis added)

My prayer is "Open the floodgates of heaven and let it rain."
Shalom.

---

275 Acts 1:8 (KJV).

276 Luke 11:1 (KJV).

277 Joel 2:25, 28–29 (NIV).

47.
LOVE AND BEAUTY

It has been said of some newborn babies that they are so ugly "only a mother could love them." That term has become a way of describing many things that appear to be ugly in the eyes of the beholder, particularly human beings. Because my profession is to attempt to create beautiful environments, it is difficult for me to see beauty in things that I know from training and experience are intrinsically ugly.

We tend to judge the choices of others by stating, "love is blind," or "I can't understand what he or she sees in her or him," while still others say they are deaf, dumb, and stupid. We say the mother is blind because she loves an ugly baby, but I have come to understand that *we are the blind ones*, because the mother sees a beauty that can only be observed through *the eyes of love*. Love sees with eyes what the natural man cannot understand, and therefore enjoys what others reject as ugly. Because we live in a society that is obsessed with "beauty," we are blinded to the splendours that only love can see.

We all know the verse from John's Gospel that states: "*For God so loved the world, that he gave His only begotten Son, that whosoever believeth in him should not perish, but have everlasting life.*"[278] I'd like to amplify the word "world" to include every living person who has ever been born or even aborted; every weak, suffering, sickly soul, every Down syndrome person, every child with cleft lip, every person regardless of age that is abandoned, abused, beaten, sexually or verbally assaulted, and every soul ravaged by sin or tormented by Satan. Despite all of this, God still sees something in us, because we were created in His image: "*And God said, Let us make man in our image, after our likeness …*"[279] But it doesn't stop there; the psalmist says that "*You saw me before I was born …*"[280]

Although I have shared this story often, it so fits this article that I ask you to forgive me for repeating it again. I was at an annual conference of the Apostolic Church when a person with a prophetic ministry came up to me, put both hands either side

---

278 John 3:16 (KJV).

279 Genesis 1:26 (KJV).

280 Psalm 139:16a (TLB).

of my face, stared compassionately into my eyes, and said, "God wants you know that He really loves you." With that he removed his hands and walked away.

That encounter changed my view of both God and myself. Like all of us when we look at our lives and see our sins and failures, I often despair and wonder how God could love me with such faults and failures. Theologically we can say that God sees us through the eyes of Christ because: "*God has given me that genuine righteousness which comes from faith in Christ,*"[281] but I believe He really does love us, even with all our quirky personalities. There are no "ugly babies" in God's eyes, because He sees beyond the obvious, loving us just as we are. Because He loves us so much, He will not leave us in our failure and sin. He sees so much incredible potential in us all that He will move "heaven and earth" to bring us to the place of change for our full destiny in Him.

Will God's love for us motivate us to be changed, or will we continue to follow our own ways and never discover the full potential and destiny for our lives? One of the scariest powers we possess is the freedom to choose. We can spit in the face of God, even deny His existence, but we do this to our own terrible eternal loss, breaking the heart of a God who has given everything possible to win us with His love. Yes, He will give strength and grace to change those ugly, sinful things in our lives, and because He loves us so much, He sees beauty where others only see ugliness.

If God then shows such love, we can—we must—show this same type of love for each other, for He has promised: "… *God's love has been poured out into our hearts through the Holy Spirit, who has been given to us.*"[282] As we choose to take that step of faith of loving each other, God's Spirit is released in us. We can then start to see beauty in each other that the natural eye cannot see. We are not like the scripture that states: "*Having eyes do you not see? And having ears, do you not hear?*"[283] We are not the blind ones; we now have eyes that see the beauty that only love can see.

Shalom.

---

281 Phillipians 3:9 (PHILLIPS).

282 Romans 5:5b (NIV).

283 Mark 8:18

48.
SILLY BOY?

I RECENTLY WENT THROUGH A PAINFUL EXPERIENCE FOR SEVERAL WEEKS WITH shingles. Despite the use of pain-killers, it consistently invaded my sleep, work, exercise, study, and prayer time. During a conversation with a friend I was asked, "Have you ever cursed yourself?" My immediate response was no, but on reflection the words "silly boy" came to mind and I realized that each time I experienced an accident, mistake, or made a misjudgement, I responded with those words. This had become my choice of "profanity." I know there are words with more sting than that, but nevertheless, it was a curse. Regardless of how "nicely" I did it, I had been unwittingly cursing myself with "silly boy." Maybe part of my shingles problem was self-inflicted.

Some use the name of Jesus and even God (or a multitude of other profane responses to life's negative experiences) to express anger, but I realize that each time we do that, the curse comes back on ourselves. My "silly" sometimes grew to "stupid," and it's not much of a step from calling me "stupid" to addressing others as "stupid." Brenda tells me that in the past I have also used the phrases "idiot Harris" and "Harris you are such a fool." The scariest thing is that I have no memory of saying such things, but that's another subject that we will look at separately.

I also see that when I curse others I curse myself too. Jesus nailed this issue when He stated, "*If you call your friend an idiot, you are in danger of being brought before the court. And if you curse him, you are in danger of the fires of hell.*"[284] Just to rub salt into my wounds, I was reminded of the Proverb that states: "*Death and life are in the power of the tongue, and those who love it will eat its fruit.*"[285] Maybe I was eating the fruit of my own words? But some comfort came from another proverb, which says, "*... But the tongue of the wise brings healing.*"[286] The Living Bible adds a little something extra: "*Some people like cutting remarks, but the words of the wise soothe and heal.*"

If this was the end of the story, I would despair, but the Holy Spirit was faithful in again reminding me of the words of Jesus: "*... bless them who curse you, do good to*

---

284 Matthew 5:22 (TLB).

285 Proverbs 18:21

286 Proverbs 12:18b

them that hate you, and pray for them which despitefully use you, and persecute you.[287]
The perfect antidote to cursing or being cursed is to bless. This isn't just good advice
or a new commandment, but healing for ourselves and the releasing of blessing to
others. Doing this will take the poison out of the curses from others and stop the
consequences we bring upon ourselves.

This experience of blessing is also linked to the forgiveness thing. We're told
that unless we forgive, God withholds forgiveness from us. If that isn't challenging
enough, we're also to bless those who have sinned against us. These are not easy
steps if we've been cruelly beaten, physically or verbally, or have seen our loved ones
beheaded by ISIS. David adds more wood to the fire when he states, "... *bless the
Lord at all times: his praise shall continually be in my mouth.*"[288] But David did not
perfect this quality. Other psalms indicate that he did not succeed in praising God at
"all times," but that doesn't change the truth of the Word.

How should I now react to the challenge of "silly boy"? Paul tells us to "*give
thanks **in all** circumstances ...*"[289] (emphasis added). That I think I can handle, but
he doesn't stop at giving thanks *in* the circumstances of life. He also tells us, "*always
giving thanks to God the Father for everything, in the name of our Lord Jesus Christ.*"[290]
What has Paul been drinking? Is this a slip of the pen? Does he live on another
planet? He reinforces his life-view in the book of Romans, where he writes: "*And we
know that all that happens to us is working for our good if we love God and are fitting into
his plans.*"[291] This is the game changer. A sovereign God is going to ultimately make
everything work for good, however bad it seems right at this moment—ISIS or no
ISIS, Nero or no Nero ... just put in your own situation.

It's from this position that we have God's perspective and can agree with His
standpoint to not only "give thanks *in* and *for* everything" but also "bless those who
curse us." We become free of the latent poison in the circumstances of life.

We're just scratching the surface with this article, and God willing we will develop this further. It will also give me more time to work on the antidote to "silly
boy," because it's still a work in process.

Shalom.

---

287 Matthew 5:44b (KJV).

288 Psalm 34:1 (KJV).

289 1 Thessalonians 5:18 (NIV).

290 Ephesians 5:20 (NIV).

291 Romans 8:28 (TLB).

49.
NO SEE UMS

THIS IS THE PERFECT NAME FOR THE TINY, BLOOD-SUCKING IRRITANTS THAT can ruin our cottage holidays. At least mosquitoes, black flies, and deer flies are big enough to sometimes be seen and heard so that evasive action can be taken, but those other creatures have the ultimate weapon of secrecy, earning them the name "No See Ums." It's only after the feeding has taken place that you become aware that they have left their calling card.

In an earlier article I revealed how I was cursing myself with phrases such as "silly boy" and even "idiot Harris." This exposure of my destructive words came following a question from a friend. As I shared this revelation with Brenda, she in turn confirmed my worst fears—I was guilty as charged, but a bigger question was raised: Why did I not see them myself? From what sort of blindness to my spoken words do I suffer that makes it obvious to others and requires outside help for me to see? Both the Prophet Isaiah and Jesus warn us of the condition: "... *ever hearing, but never understanding; ever seeing, but never perceiving.*"[292] I have often wondered how that could be, but now I faced a classic case of the "No See Ums."

I do understand that in a similar sense I only see what my brain expects to see with my natural eyesight, demonstrated in experiences like looking for my glasses when in fact they are perched on my head, or my cell phone when it's in front of me. The same principle of only seeing what our mind expects us to see applies to our behaviour. These issues are obvious to others, but to us, they are "No See Ums."

Jesus also cautioned about judging, because although we see the faults in others, we are afflicted with a two-by-four piece of lumber in our own eyes. He advised that we remove that one first. The question then becomes: How can we remove what we don't see, but others do? In my case it required someone caring enough about me to risk asking the right questions with the hope that I was open to learning and being corrected. Denial of the truth deceives and prevents us from any form of change, as illustrated by those trapped in addictions. What we don't seem to realize is that our repeated words and actions are "addictions."

---

292   Isaiah 6:9b (NIV).

Scripture talks about *"speaking the truth in love"*[293] to each other. Just as neglecting to correct our children is considered a lack of love, so likewise for each other. Do we love others enough to risk sharing what we see for their sake? This is not an open invitation to play sheriff, and if we feel this gives us the right to confront each other then we have the wrong motive. One of the reasons Christians must be part of a local congregation is to encourage each other to become more like Christ. Fellowship and relationship are vital parts of being the body of Christ. It is part of God's method and plan for character change.

God is determined to see us conformed to the image of His Son and has been working on us before and after our *"born again"*[294] experience. Jesus was talking about spiritual eyes when He pointed out that seeing the Kingdom of God requires eyes that can perceive and understand this different type of kingdom.

Part of the work of the Holy Spirit is to reveal those things that need our repentance and change, but choosing to change remains our decision. James tells us: *"Admit your faults to one another and pray for each other so that you may be healed. The earnest prayer of a righteous man has great power and wonderful results."*[295] The humility to share the failures we observe in ourselves releases others to speak into our lives about those things we do not see. Here is the word of encouragement for us all, whatever our age. It took God eighty years to bring Moses to a place where he could be the man to deliver Israel from Egyptian slavery. All he learned while shepherding sheep in the wilderness became wisdom for what lay ahead.

PRAYER: "Open the eyes of my heart, Lord, that I may see what needs to be changed and receive insight from those who care for me. Grant me the grace to change so that I become more like Christ."

Shalom.

---

293   Ephesians 4:15 (NIV).
294   John 3:3 (NIV).
295   James 5:16 (TLB).

50.
TRAFFIC LIGHTS

Have you ever experienced the frustration of sitting behind someone at a left turn signal when it changes to "turn" but they remain stationary? Every second feels like an eternity. The adrenalin rises, and you share ways of encouragement by laying on the horn accompanied by a little personal verbal support, which of course they cannot hear! Life is like that. At times we need to have the brakes on, and other times the foot needs to be on the accelerator. Traffic lights are one of those times, and they form a perfect illustration for one of the most important principles of life—when to stop, when to go, and recognizing when and how to respond. There can be serious consequences for ourselves and others at left turn signals if we fail to be alert to the instructions of those signals—being "T" boned, "T" boning someone else, or just delaying traffic.

Scripture is like that too. Sometimes we are told to *"Be **still**, and know that I am God ..."*[296] (emphasis added), while at others we are instructed to *"... **run** with patience the race that is set before us."*[297] God *"... also hath **ceased** from his own works ..."*[298] but we are to *"**strive** to enter through the narrow door ..."*[299] (emphasis added). Jesus leaves the disciples with the command to *"**GO** therefore and make disciples of all the nations"*[300] (emphasis added), but then tells them, *"...**wait** for the promise of the Father ..."*[301] (emphasis added). Doing the right thing at the right time leads to success, but doing the right thing at the wrong time results in failure.

Despite the clear instructions of the left turn arrow, people still get killed turning left. When we do not get God's timing right for the seasons of our life, it not only impacts ourselves, but also a multitude of others. For the Children of Israel in the wilderness there was a time to follow God's instruction to enter and take the Promised Land, but fear paralyzed them at the left turn signal. Instead, they later decided

---

296   Psalm 46:10a (KJV).

297   Hebrews 12:1 (KJV).

298   Hebrews 4:10 (KJV).

299   Luke 13:24a.

300   Matthew 28:19 (KJV).

301   Acts 1:4b (KJV).

to go when the lights changed to red, and they got "T" boned. The consequence was a forty-year wandering in the wilderness, and none of them entered the Promised Land except Joshua and Caleb, who obeyed God's timing.

Solomon tells us that *"There is an appointed **time** for everything"*[302] (emphasis added), a time to turn left and a time to remain stopped. Jesus rebuked Martha because she was angry at her sister, who sat at Jesus' feet listening to His words. Martha thought she should be working. I experience the same rebuke when I fail to "sit at His feet." During times of prayer, I sometimes receive insights and revelations about the things of God, and my immediate reaction is to rush to capture them on paper. An almost audible voice calls out, saying, "Stop. This is our time together." I confess I have done the same with Brenda many times—doing, instead of stopping to listen. This type of response reveals my self-centred life view. Even though I may be doing something good, it's based on my decision to turn left on a red light, with me suffering all the consequences. They may not be as dramatic as being "T" boned, but they impact our relationships with both God and each other.

God is the author of perfect timing and precision, which is confirmed in the perfectly functioning universe. It is said of Jesus that *"... when the fullness of **time** came, God sent forth his Son ..."*[303] (emphasis added)—not a day too early or a day too late, but right on time. Examine the perfection of timing surrounding His death, resurrection, and then the outpouring of the Holy Spirit at Pentecost. This is the stuff Bible students devour, but the real application is for our own lives to be like Christ, who said, *"I do nothing on my own initiative, but I speak these things as the Father has taught Me."*[304] God has given us both the letter (the Bible) and the Holy Spirit to guide us so that we can confidently live our lives and not turn left on a red light.

The Psalmist states: *"My **times** are in thy hand ..."*[305] (emphasis added), but we need to make sure that we continue to learn to follow the leading of the Holy Spirit and the scripture so that we become more like Jesus in character, works, and timing. The challenge is to develop our ears to hear: *"Whoever has ears, let them hear what the Spirit says to the churches ..."*[306] and do it. I have recently taken to paraphrase the Lord's Prayer as "Your Kingdom come now, *continuosly* in me and this

---

302   Ecclesiastes 3:1a.
303   Galatians 4:4
304   John 8:28b
305   Psalm 31:15a (KJV).
306   Revelation 2:7a (NIV).

church; Your will be done now, *continuosly* in me and this church." I want to learn to flow with God's purpose in God's perfect timing.

Shalom.

51.
TWO TREES

LIFE IS A CONTINUOUS STREAM OF CHOICES, AND IN EVERY WAKING MOMENT WE are called to choose. Some of those decisions prove to be wise, others successful, and some failures, but most habitually pass us by—apparently without notice. The reality is that none are benign, because everything we do has consequences.

The book of Genesis tells the story of two trees, one named the tree of life and the other the tree of the knowledge of good and bad. Our first parents were warned that the consequence of eating the fruit of the second tree was death. Regrettably, with the help of some outside influence, they chose the latter and, as they say, "the rest is history." Tragically, the consequences of that decision infected all their progeny with the same fruit—the DNA of sin.

When our lives are controlled by choices made from the fruit of the tree of the knowledge of good and bad, we cannot escape the outcome of "death." Mankind relies on reason and knowledge for the understanding of life's experiences. It has been proven that all endeavours using this process to return to the paradise of the garden are doomed to failure, because they eventually all end in death. Every person, community, city, nation, or empire has fallen for the same reason. Every attempt at finding the "gods" through religion by this method is fatally flawed, because only the tree of life has the key to life.

Karl Marx, the Jewish author of communism, believed that exterminating the aristocracy would pave the way for the common man to produce a paradise, but instead the fruit was actually a new form of hell. Charles Darwin, by the same process, arrived at a theory that every living thing evolved from a single cell. Now all philosophy and understanding of man is so completely based on this "origin of the species" that even the idea of "creation" cannot be mentioned in the educational system. In some circles using the word "creation" is worse than being contagious with Ebola!

Christianity has not been immune to this approach. Most Reformation church denominations have fallen into what is called "higher criticism," where the supernatural, miracles, the Virgin Birth, the resurrection, and the Bible are debunked. Within evangelical and charismatic congregations, a similar development occurs. Scripture is studied only from the perspective of the tree of knowledge, even though

Jesus clearly said, "... *no one can see the kingdom of God unless they are born again.*"[307] That is the tree of life. Even "end times" theories can fall into the same category, because "*knowledge makes proud but love builds up.*"[308]

This is not to ignore "knowledge," because scripture states that "*my people are destroyed from lack of knowledge,*"[309] but that knowledge must be seen through the eyes of the tree of life. It is from the "knowledge only" approach that we have birthed doctrines that divide us, such as in whose name and how many times we should be baptized, or whether speaking in tongues is the only sign of being filled with the Holy Spirit, or that the pre-tribulation version of the second coming of Christ is the only correct interpretation of end time events.

The consequence of restored New Testament truths brings life, new understanding, and revelation, but they are not well received by the establishment and inevitably cause division and the birthing of new movements. Yet these truths appear to conflict with the prayer of Jesus: "*... that they may be one, as we are one ...,*"[310] but in reality, they are the breath of new life to the church and a sign of her health and vitality. If our unity is based purely on doctrine or the institution to which we adhere, then we are eating from the tree of the knowledge of good and bad. Becoming one is an act of our hearts to follow Christ's demand to love one another to the same degree that he loves us.

Now this is the tree of life: "*... let us love one another, for love comes from God. Everyone who loves has been born of God and knows God. Whoever does not love does not know God, because God is love.*"[311] This is the unity that enables diverse people, personalities, cultures, and those from various religious backgrounds to become one. "But," you may say, "what is this 'love' of which John is speaking, and can you qualify it?"

Paul lists at least sixteen attributes of this type of love:

Love is patient, love is kind. It does not envy, it does not boast, it is not proud. It does not dishonor others, it is not self-seeking, it is not easily angered, it keeps no record of wrongs. Love does not delight in evil but rejoices with the truth

---

307   John 3:3b (NIV).

308   1 Corinthians 8:1 (ONMB)

309   Hosea 4:6 (NIV).

310   John 17:22b (NIV).

311   1 John 4:7–8 (NIV).

[is glad when truth prevails with all men]. It always protects, always trusts, always hopes, always perseveres. Love never fails.[312]

This is eating from the tree of life, where we become one with each other. In the words of Moses:

> *... I have set before you life and death, blessings and curses. Now choose life, so that you and your children may live and that you may love the Lord your God, listen to his voice and hold fast to him. For the Lord is your life.*[313]

Shalom.

---

312 1 Corinthians 13:4–8 (NIV).

313 Deuteronomy 30:19 (NIV).

52.
TO EAT OR NOT TO EAT—
THAT IS THE QUESTION

First, my apologies to William Shakespeare for taking the liberty of misquoting a speech from Hamlet, but it expresses the same principle of exercising our free will. As the offspring of Adam, the infection of flawed DNA that was passed down by our parents has compromised our ability to freely choose. Our "free will" is not as free as we think. When we live at the level of our five natural senses, we become slaves to our desires.

Genesis tells us that "... *the Lord God formed the man from the dust of the ground and breathed into his nostrils the breath of life, and the man became a living being.*"[314] The decision to live the full expression of his five senses and the desires of his soul led King Henry VIII of England to eat and drink his way to an overburdening weight of four hundred pounds. Among the consequences of his compulsion were the destroyed lives of his six wives and a premature death at age fifty-six, all because his freedom to choose said "he could."

For the first time in history we in the Western world have the ability to follow his example. We have at our disposal more food and drink than we need in order to satisfy the cravings of our body and soul, and we do it just because "we can." One out of every two adults are obese, as is one out of every six children. One-third of the world is overweight, with the USA leading the way.[315] Why? Because "we can."

Type 2 diabetes is so common that it is estimated the 422,000,000 people worldwide now suffer from the disease because of the Western-type diet.

Excess consumption of sugar results in type 2 diabetes, heart disease, stroke, gall bladder, liver issues, high blood pressure, sleep apnea,

---

314   Genesis 2:7 (NIV).

315   OECD, "Obesity Update 2017," https://politics.ucsc.edu/undergraduate/chicago%20style%20
        guide.pdf (accessed May 11, 2018).

infertility, respiratory problems, colon, breast, and endometrial cancers and Alzheimer's.[316]

We are suffering from lifestyle diseases that only the "King Henrys" of the past had to face.

What should we then do as Christians? Should we develop a list of things we are allowed to eat and drink and another for those from which we must abstain? Do we ban visits to fast food restaurants and certain foods? Do we become vegetarians? All of the above are possibilities, but making them a law defeats the issue of exercising our free will.

Joining a monastery or becoming a celibate priest will not eliminate the five senses or the desires of the soul. This is a battle we must all face individually by personal choice. We cannot put our solutions on others by legislating them without removing our most precious, God-given commodity of free will. That was demonstrated in US history by their failed attempt to stop the negative consequences of alcohol by legislating it during the 1920s with prohibition. The 1920 ban failed because flawed human nature found a way to circumvent the law.

One of the curses of the sin nature is that we are prone to addictions of both soul and body. So how then can we be delivered from the chains of poisons that can kill us? As Christians we are not left alone with our problems. The Scriptures are full of promises of help and deliverance, such as with the Apostle Paul's "thorn in the flesh." God's reply to his request to have it removed was: "… *My grace is sufficient for you, for my power is made perfect in weakness.*"[317] Paul declared, "*For I can do everything through Christ, who gives me strength.*"[318]

The process of deliverance can be instant, but most often it is a work that replaces one negative thing with a positive, God-centric one. Jesus tells the parable of the man delivered from a demon; the house is swept clean, but the demon returns to the empty home with nine of his colleagues in tow.[319] Nature abhors a vacuum in every area of life.

These are the personal battles we all face to some degree or another, but because we have a weakness or success in one area, can we turn our opinions into rules

---

316 Bethany Fong, R.D., "Damaging Effects of Too Much Sugar," *Livestrong.com*, Last modified October 3, 2017, https://www.livestrong.com/article/144711-damaging-effects-of-too-much-sugar-in-diet/.

317 2 Corinthians 12:9a (NIV).

318 Philippians 4:13 (NLT).

319 Luke 11:14–26.

and expect others to live by them? *"And if another believer is distressed by what you eat, you are not acting in love if you eat it."*[320] This means that the motive by which we respond to each other's weaknesses should be love for that person: *"For the Kingdom of God is not a matter of what we eat or drink, but of living a life of goodness and peace and joy in the Holy Spirit.*[321] Does that mean it's a free for all, because eating and drinking are not part of the kingdom? Not in the least. Scripture also states: *"… whatever you do, do it all for to the glory of God."*[322] If we are controlled by addictions, this is not for God's glory and we need deliverance.

The balance is found here:

> *Let us therefore make every effort to do what leads to peace and to mutual edification. Do not destroy the work of God for the sake of food. All food is clean, but it is wrong for a man to eat anything that causes someone else anyone to stumble.*[323]

The decision to abstain or participate is left to the individual based on their attitude of love for the other, not by a rule or law—as good and wise as it may appear. We enter a dangerous minefield when we establish rules outside the mandate of the three laws of love revealed to us by Christ. Paul also cautions us in Galatians: *"All who rely on the works of the law are under a curse …"*[324] We can quickly move into legalism when we add good rules and laws to suit each new situation. These then are "works of the flesh," which only bear fruit of division and strife.

Deciding "to eat or not to eat" is everyone's responsibility, and not just from their own personal standpoint but motivated by love, which means considering how that decision impacts others.

Shalom.

---

320   Romans 14:15a (NLT).

321   Romans 14:17 (NLT).

322   1 Corinthians 10:31 (NIV).

323   Romans 14:19–20 (NIV).

324   Galatians 3:10a (NIV).

53.
GOD'S GYM—I KNOW MORE THAN I AM

THIS IS NOW APRIL, AND MOST WHO SIGNED UP TO JOIN A GYM IN JANUARY HAVE lapsed and are back on the old treadmill of unhealthy living. It's one of the inherent character weaknesses of human nature. We know what we should be doing for our physical and spiritual welfare, but we don't have what it takes to persevere to achieve it. In that sense, "we know more than we are." Just as joining the gym is the right first step to improving our physical health, receiving Christ as Lord and Saviour is the essential first step to inheriting eternal life. Both decisions require a procedure that will turn one act into a lifestyle.

Regular attendance at the gym will develop at least two benefits; the first results in a healthier body and the second in the strengthening of our character in the virtue of perseverance. The same applies to our walk with God. Regular spiritual disciplines will result in a new lifestyle. All Christians are aware of the simple exercises of daily prayer, reading the Bible, and regular attendance at a local congregation. Nevertheless, despite the seemingly obvious process, statistics indicate that many Christians living under the assumption that a weekly visit to church is sufficient to maintain good spiritual health fail to follow the simple program. This is no more possible than expecting that a weekly visit to a gym will successfully maintain our physical health.

There is often an excitement, a euphoria, during the first days at the gym, but soon the demands of family, work, and leisure—coupled with the pain in muscles you didn't know you had—demand your attention. The enthusiasm diminishes, so with a promise to make up for lost time, you skip a day or two, but the days turn into a week and the week into several more until you convince yourself that "it was too demanding" and you quit. The Christian life follows a similar pattern, but the consequences of failure and quitting are even greater than failing to maintain our health; we are playing with our eternal destiny.

God's purpose for us is to become sons of God: *"But as many as received him, to them gave he power to become the sons of God ..."*[325]—just like Jesus. That means moving from a position of maintaining a spiritual life to allowing the Holy Spirit to

---

325 John 1:12 (KJV).

transform us into "the image of His Son." The daily exercises of prayer and scripture reading are the necessary foundational disciplines that enable us to develop a God-centred lifestyle.

> Therefore, everyone who hears these words of mine and puts them into practice is like a wise man who built his house on the rock … yet it did not fall, because it had its foundation on the rock. But everyone who hears these words of mine and does not put them into practice is like a foolish man who built his house on sand. The rain came down, the streams rose, and the winds blew and beat upon that house, and it fell with a great crash."[326]

This is what "building your house on the rock and not on the sand" means, and that building enables us to remain standing, regardless of when and what form the tests take.

This may all sound like "blood, sweat, and tears," but those who have pursued a healthy lifestyle of exercise will tell you that the body's release of pleasure endorphins produces the "runner's high" that comes from pressing beyond the maintenance experience. As Christians, we can enjoy a similar occurrence as we persevere beyond maintenance: "… *weeping may endure for a night, but **joy cometh in the morning**"*[327] (emphasis added). We have the ability to experience the blessing of God's presence: "*For the Kingdom of God is not a matter of eating and drinking, but of righteousness, peace, and **joy in the Holy Spirit**"*[328] (emphasis added).

The same thing happens in the spiritual realm; we get a "runner's high" if we persevere. The goal is to turn these encounters into habitual behaviour patterns that changes our character and enables us to "… [come] *unto a perfect man, unto the measure of the stature of the fullness of Christ.*"[329] The good news is that:

> *His divine power has given us everything we need for a godly life through our knowledge of him who called us by his own glory and goodness. Through these he has given us his very great and precious promises, so that through them you may participate in the divine nature, having escaped the corruption in the world caused by evil desires. For this very reason, **make every effort** to add to*

---

326   Matthew 7:24–27 (NIV).

327   Psalm 30:5 (KJV).

328   Romans 14:17 (NIV).

329   Ephesians 4:13b (KJV).

your faith goodness; and to goodness, knowledge; and to knowledge, self-control; and to self-control, perseverance; and to perseverance, godliness; and to godliness, mutual affection; and to mutual affection, love … For if you do these things, you will never stumble, and you will receive a rich welcome into the eternal kingdom of our Lord and Savior Jesus Christ."[330] (emphasis added)

If what is being described challenges you, then be encouraged. We don't attend the gym alone. This is not a "lone ranger" exercise but a team experience where we encourage, support, and provoke one another to love, so that *all* may reach the goals of God's destiny for each of our lives. God provides both a coach and power equipment: "*Howbeit when he, the Spirit of truth, is come, he will guide you into all truth: for he will not speak of himself; but whatsoever he shall hear, that shall he speak: and he will shew you things to come.*"[331] Christ also promises: "*But you will receive power when the Holy Spirit comes on you …*"[332]

Shalom.

---

330   2 Peter 1:3–7, 10b–11 (NIV).

331   John 16:13 (NIV).

332   Acts 1:8a (NIV).

54.
OUR NAKEDNESS

"He opened the door of the tent and there lay his father, drunk and stark naked on the floor. He rushed from the tent to tell his brothers what he had seen" (Genesis 9:22, paraphrased). This account describes Noah lying naked in a drunken sleep, even though scripture portrays him as "... *a righteous man, blameless among the people of the time, and he walked faithfully with God.*"[333]

While Ham disgraced his father, Noah's other two sons, Shem and Japheth, honoured him despite his failure. In order to not look upon his nakedness, they entered the tent backwards then placed a sheet over his exposed body. There is something in the nature of man that wants to feast on the failures of others. Much of the content in our daily diet comes from the media appealing to this perverted appetite. The more important the person, the greater the news value when their sins are revealed to public view. Politicians, preachers, and celebrities are fodder for a media so hungry for scandal, they became complicit in the death of Princess Diana.

As Christians, we are not immune to the temptation to feed on this perverted appetite, particularly in the church setting. When we hear of some successful preacher caught in a transgression, the temptation is to feast on the flesh like vultures. What tantalizing opportunities are presented to us! "*Gossip is a dainty morsel eaten with great relish.*"[334]

The story of Noah describes the curse that he spoke over his son, Ham, when he exposed his father's nakedness, and so it is with us—we bring a curse on ourselves when we reveal the failures of others. How can that be? Let me explain. I am not suggesting we conceal our sins ... quite the contrary. We confess them but understand that it is the responsibility of the sinner to do the confessing—not anyone else. When we hear of their transgressions, it is we who are in danger. We have to learn how to deal with garbage in a God-honouring way; how we handle this toxic information determines our own destiny in Christ.

As the saying goes, "We are what we eat." This sort of food will infect our lives in the same way as a dose of Salmonella. It is therefore wise to sometimes stop people

---

333 Genesis 6:9 (NIV).
334 Proverbs 26:22 (TLB).

from sharing the poison. Paul tells us that *"Love does not delight in evil …,"*[335] or as J.B. Phillips puts it: *"… gloat over other men's sins."*[336] Sometimes it may be better to not know, or even want to know, the sins of others. We face the temptation of judging them, and we always judge from our own strengths and standards. Jesus warned us: *"For in the same way you judge others, you will be judged, and with the measure you use, it will be measured to you."*[337] This is a double-edged sword that needs to be kept in its scabbard. We can't see the full picture. Only God has the key, and He says that He will judge righteously. Scripture states: *"Your own soul is nourished when you are kind; it is destroyed when you are cruel."*[338]

Though we don't tolerate sin, this is the advice we are given: *"… love covers over a multitude of sins."*[339] This speaks to our attitude, so remember: *"for all have sinned and fall short of the glory of God."*[340] God is in the saving, delivering, healing, and restoration business, not the demolition and destruction business. He has determined to see us conformed to the image of His Son. Paul tells us that *"… if a Christian is overcome by some sin, you who are godly should gently and humbly help him back onto the right path, remembering that next time it might be one of you who is in the wrong."*[341]

When Jesus was crucified, He faced the ultimate humiliation of being hung naked in public. In our day where nakedness is commonplace, it is hard for us to grasp the full extent of this act. We are told that He was exposed naked so that our nakedness could be covered by Him. He became the substitute for us all; therefore, let us be merciful in dealing with each other. When we are found guilty and our nakedness is exposed, we need others to be our Shem and Japheth, not looking at the failures but entering into our lives in order to cover our nakedness with the blanket of love.

Shalom.

---

335   1 Corinthians 13:6 (NIV).

336   J.B. Phillips, *Letters to Young Churches: A Translation of the New Testament Epistles* (London: Geoffrey Bless, 1954), 58.

337   Matthew 7:2 (NIV).

338   Proverbs 11:17 (TLB).

339   1 Peter 4:8b (NIV).

340   Romans 3:23 (NIV).

341   Galatians 6:1 (TLB).

55.
THE TIPPING POINT

RECENTLY A US PRESIDENTIAL DECREE WAS ISSUED DEMANDING THAT ALL states make provision for special bathroom facilities for those who consider themselves "transgender." Despite the fact that the declaration was both unilateral and unconstitutional, the method of enforcement was to withhold health and education funding from any states refusing to cooperate. The purpose of this article is not to examine either the moral or political merits of the bill, but to observe the unique power of the few to bring about such a dramatic change for the majority.

What was the tipping point that enabled the President to authorise such a decision? This was not one isolated incident, but part of a series of decisions removing all constraints inherited from the Judeo/Christian code of moral behaviour. From conception to abortion, the normalization of multiple sexual preferences and relationships, common law relationships, and now the authority to end life prematurely, are all part of the groundswell that made such a decision possible.

The good news is that the principle of the few impacting the majority is not exclusive to those who are intent on destroying the moral fibre of a nation. The history of the Christian church is filled with times of revival, of "tipping points" that have helped change the world for the better. The freedoms, justice, education, hospitals, and ideals of trust and honesty in government and business, as well as some of the things we take for granted, are the fruit of a minority deeply committed to seeing *"your kingdom come, your will be done, on earth as it is in heaven."*[342]

How can so few impact the many to lead us to the tipping point" of revival? Because God has given us in Christ the keys to life, death, and eternity, we must first be totally committed to God's full agenda for our personal and corporate lives. It has been recorded that God's man, Evan Roberts, who led the Welsh Revival was only interested in glorifying God and seeing people saved. He didn't have a personal agenda. His vision was simple and God-given, and his passion was to be totally obedient. He was not alone in his desire for a move of God, but God used Evan Roberts as the tipping point, even though he was only twenty-seven with limited education. He was instrumental in changing a nation, and so impacted the world that we still

---

342   Matthew 6:10 (NIV).

enjoy the fruit today. There are no limits. Whether young as Evan or as old as Moses, the world has yet to see what God can do with a group of people with this type of dedication to His purposes.

God has revealed in His Word how we as a congregation can become that tipping point for our locality:

> If my people, who are called by my name, will humble themselves and pray and seek my face and turn from their wicked ways, then will I hear from heaven, and will forgive their sin and will **heal their land**."[343] (emphasis added)

He has been dealing with us by calling for a deep repentance, an appeal to be humble and a cry that we love each other the same way Jesus loves us. The question is: Will we heed the call? Will we be like Evan Roberts, who called out from the depth of his soul: "Bend us oh Lord!"[344]

We have the keys, but to enable the Holy Spirit to use them, we must follow the way of the cross—death of self and total dedication to God's plans: "For it is time for judgment to begin with God's household; and if it begins with us, what will the outcome be for those who do not obey the gospel of God?"[345]

When can we expect this "tipping point" to occur? The disciples asked a similar question of Christ moments before His ascension:

> "... Lord, are you at this time going to restore the kingdom to Israel?" He said to them: "It is not for you to know the times or dates the Father has set by his own authority. But you will receive power when the Holy Spirit comes upon you; and you will be my witnesses ... "[346]

Jesus declares that the timing is in God's hands. Our part is to obey the word Jesus gave, and this will coincide with God's timing.

We are asked to follow the pattern;

> And when the day of Pentecost was fully come [timing] they were all in one accord [unity] in one place [location together]. And suddenly [tipping point] there came a sound from heaven as of a rushing mighty wind, and it filled the house

---

343 2 Chronicles 7:14 (NIV).

344 Rick Joyner, The World Aflame (Charlotte, North Carolina: Morning Star Publications 1993), 30.

345 1 Peter 4:17 (NIV).

346 Acts 1:6–8 (NIV).

where they were sitting. And there appeared unto them cloven tongues like as of fire, and it sat upon each of them. And they were all filled with the Holy Ghost, and began to speak with other tongues, as the Spirit gave them utterance.[347]

Nothing like this had ever happened before, so the accusation that they were drunk seemed a likely answer to these manifestations. When God interacts with His creation there is diversity in each involvement, and we have been warned that what we believe is coming will not be like any other previous move of God, so keep your hearts and minds open for the coming tipping point.

Shalom.

---

347   Acts 2:1–4 (KJV).

56.
MIND GAMES

HERE I AM AGAIN, DISTURBED SLEEP AND TRYING TO PRAY BUT STILL TASTING THE strange flavours left by broken dream patterns. My mind is seething with thoughts, like a TV convertor gone crazy and skipping wildly through a thousand channels; nevertheless, I am determined to pray so I can bring this cacophony to order and command my mind to *"Be still, and know that I am God ..."*[348] My mind, however, seems to have a mind of its own. I call out, "Who is in charge here?" But my mind continues to race in wild confusion. So who is in charge here, anyway, and why does it seem as though my mind is totally confused?

If you have never had a similar experience, then this article is not for you. But I am convinced that because all are children of Adam, we will share similar challenges to varying degrees. If at times it appears that the mind is not under our control, then how do we unplug the machine? How do we make sense of those apparently senseless dreams, and what about the ones with the signature of God all over them? *"And it shall come to pass afterward, that I will pour out my spirit upon all flesh; and your sons and daughters shall prophesy, your old men shall dream dreams, your young men shall see visions."*[349] My age now fully qualifies me for the dreams bit ... at least while I'm still here.

One of the consequences of the fall is the apparent disconnect between our souls and bodies. Adam's sin fractured the unity of man's tri-part being (spirit, soul, and body, as described in 1 Thessalonians 5:23) by reversing the order of control. Rather than the spirit and soul uniting to call the shots, it's the body and soul in collusion against the spirit that's actually running the show, unless one is "born again"[350] of God's Spirit. Regeneration then puts us in a war zone of our own making. There is, however good news: *"And the peace of God, which passeth all understanding* [the mind], *shall keep your hearts* [soul] *and minds through Christ Jesus."*[351] The OMB translation says it this way: *"on Christ Jesus,"* while the Living Bible uses the words *"as you trust in."*

---

348   Psalm 46:10a (KJV).
349   Joel 2:28 (KJV).
350   John 3:3.
351   Philippians 4:7 (KJV).

We surrendered our authority and order at the fall, but in Christ they have both been restored. That restoration of divine order enables us to speak to the mountain by faith[352] and demand these wild thoughts to come into God's order. Like unruly kids, they may resist the word of command at first, but as we continue calling them to order they must eventually surrender to the Spirit. All of this is conditional; if we knowingly or unknowingly have secret sin agendas, those agendas cause us to relinquish our personal authority over those thoughts and give them permission to continue.

As the saying goes "garbage in/garbage out." We must discipline the access door to our minds by feeding it with good material; "*Finally, brethren, whatsoever things are true, whatsoever things are honest, whatsoever things are just ... whatsoever things are lovely ... if there be any virtue, and if there be any praise, think on these things.*"[353]

We need the process of sleep for many reasons, one of which is to "do the filing" from the day's business. Even though it never sleeps, God has designed a unique method of vacuuming the brain in the slumber process. Just as computers have a "cleaner app," and the body a waste removal system, so the brain has a cleaning mechanism. One of the worst forms of torture is sleep deprivation, because lack of sleep stops the cleanup process from working. The consequence is that we suffocate in our own garbage and become totally disoriented.

What shall we then say to these mind games? Shall we let them rule us, or will we take authority in the name of Jesus over them? Will we as much as is possible determine who and what goes into our minds? Peter states:

> *His divine power has given us everything we need for a godly life through our knowledge of him… Through these he has given us his very great and precious promises, so that through them you may participate in the divine nature [our part] ... For this very reason make every effort to add to your faith goodness; and to goodness, knowledge; and to knowledge, self-control; and to self-control, perseverance; and to perseverance, godliness; and to godliness, mutual affection; and to mutual affection, love. For if you posses these qualities in increasing measure, they will keep you from being ineffective and unproductive in your knowledge of our Lord Jesus Christ.*[354]

Part of the eternal promise is that there will be no more night, because God Himself will be the light. One must assume that there will be no more sleep or need

---

352   Luke 11:23

353   Philippians 4:8 (KJV).

354   2 Peter 1:3 (NIV).

for it, but until that day, we must do battle with the dreams and mind games of our fallen nature. But be encouraged, because with all the equipment we have been given to overcome, we can be victors because of what Jesus has done for us!

Shalom.

57.
UNKNOWN TERRITORY

WHETHER WE ARE CONSCIOUSLY AWARE OF IT OR NOT, LIFE IS A DAILY journey into the unknown. The regular patterns of sunrise and sunset can lull us into believing that life will continue "ad infinitum." However, this is far from the truth. Believing a lie makes us blind, deaf, and dumb to the uniqueness of each day. The consequence is that we are taken by surprise when we experience an event outside our perceived norm. A recent example is the U.K.'s decision to exit the European Union. The unintended consequence was that the global stock markets reacted like a deranged Las Vegas gambler. The world's economic decisions depend on a predicable outcome and have no moral or political motivation.

On a personal level, we are depending on our health, job, pension, relationships, and even our very life as if they were guaranteed to remain as they are, totally undisturbed. Jesus warned: *"So don't be anxious about tomorrow. God will take care of your tomorrow too. Live one day at a time."*[355] This doesn't mean that we aren't to plan for tomorrow; stocking our freezers for a rainy day is wisdom, but remember the parable of the farmer—he built larger barns to store his successful harvest, only to find that *"this very night your soul is required of you."*[356]

We have incorporated this expectation of predictability into our church life, and it has stifled our expectation of embracing the new and unknown. We have atrophied our faith; anything that does not follow "the tradition of the elders" is heresy. Jesus faced the same attitude; everything He said was received with unbelief by the incredulous hearers.

As a congregation we are seeking God for what we call a "revival," or "move of God," but recent prophetic words have cautioned that "this next move will be different from past revivals." This now presents a challenge. With the exception of gleaning understanding from the principles undergirding each demonstration of God's mercy, we cannot rely on the books and studies of previous "moves of God." Even Jesus followed this pattern in His sermon on the mount, where He taught the principles of truth behind each part of the Old Covenant Law. He explained that adultery

---

355 Matthew 6:34 (TLB).

356 Luke 12:20

doesn't have to happen as a physical act to be sin. He took it to a deeper level when He said that it's still adultery when it occurs in the heart and mind.

Joshua was given the mantle of authority to lead the children of Israel across the Jordan into the Promised Land, but the land of "milk and honey" was full of warlike tribes that had to be defeated. God warned him: "*You have never been where we are going now ...*"[357] It was a major experience of moving entirely by faith into the unknown. The body of Christ faces such a situation at this moment in history. There are giants of militant atheism, Islam, and the gay community, but God declares: "*The earth is the Lord's ... the world, and they that dwell therein.*"[358]

We stand at the edge of our "Jordan River," and we are to follow the revelation of how to cross this river when it floods. It was an act of faith when Joshua instructed the priests to carry the Ark of the Covenant over the river: "*When the priests who are carrying the Ark touch the water with their feet, the river will stop flowing as though held back by a dam, and will pile up as though against an invisible wall!*"[359] This is the blend of God's purposes and man's act of obedience to walk in faith by stepping into the unknown: "*and the priests who were carrying the Ark stood on dry ground in the middle of the Jordan and waited as all the people passed by.*"[360]

We are entering an unknown, volatile future, but we have the Ark of the Covenant with us—Christ Himself, our Joshua, who will lead us into the promised land of His Kingdom. Yes, there are enemies of the Kingdom of God, but as John states: "*... greater is he that is in you, than he that is in the world.*"[361]

Get ready; the call is coming, for "*... the Lord hath given you the land ...*"[362]

Shalom.

---

357 Joshua 3:4 (TLB).
358 Psalm 24:1 (KJV).
359 Joshua 3:13a (TLB).
360 Joshua 3:17 (TLB).
361 1 John 4:4b (KJV).
362 Joshua 2:9 (KJV).

58.
BLIND AND DEAF

THERE SITTING ON THE DOOR OF THE TOTALLY WHITE FRIDGE WAS MY grandson's totally black, lonely business card. I had asked Brenda for his email address, and she informed me that it was "on the fridge." It's our custom to put any business cards of note on the side of the fridge, and as a dutiful husband, that's where I looked. In this case, Brenda had broken the system by placing it on the front several weeks ago. I can't think how many times I have opened that fridge door but never "saw" that black card there.

This is a classic case of the phenomena of "only seeing what the brain lets you see." Our brains are part of our decision-making process and are encased in the darkness of a thick-boned skull. In order to provide us with understanding, it takes the information received from the five senses and "interprets" each encounter through our library of past experience and knowledge. My brain had filed our custom of only putting the business cards on the side of the fridge but had no library reference of one on the front; consequently, I was blind to any other option.

This may appear unusual to our understanding, but our ears follow the same pattern. We only "hear" what our brains can interpret. There needs to be a reference point so that the brain can translate an experience of sound into a reality. This becomes an excellent excuse for spouses to be "deaf" to their partners! If you're struggling with this concept, then an additional illustration may help. Similar to a camera, there is a hole in the centre of the eyeball that allows an observed image to fall onto the retina. Since the brain interprets what is seen, there should be a hole in every image, but amazingly, the brain creatively paints in the missing parts from the surrounding information.

The reason for this lengthy dialogue is to help us understand the truth behind the words spoken by Jesus to Nicodemus:

> Very truly I tell you, no one can **see** the kingdom of God unless they are born again ... Flesh gives birth to flesh, but the Spirit gives birth to spirit ... we speak of what we know, and we testify to what we have **seen**"[363] (emphasis added)

---

363   John 3:3, 6, 11a (NIV).

The blindness experience isn't just for the eyes and ears; it is also a blindness of the heart. When I looked for the black card on the white fridge door *after* being informed of its location, I saw it! All facts, truth, knowledge, and revelation are processed by the same method; our "eyes" have to be opened from outside ourselves, and in my case, I needed Brenda to give me the key.

Despite Jesus' miracles and authoritative teaching of the Kingdom of God, the scribes and Pharisees were blind and deaf to what He said about Himself. In His criticism of them He quoted Isaiah: "*Though seeing, they do not see; though hearing, they do not hear or understand.*"[364] He also told His disciples: "*But when the Comforter is come, whom I will send unto you from the Father, even the **Spirit of truth**, which proceedeth from the Father, he shall testify of me …*"[365] (emphasis added). God's word to King David was: "*I will instruct thee and teach thee in the way which thou shalt go: I will guide thee with mine eye.*"[366] God wants to reveal Himself to us.

Part of our experience of "seeing and hearing" can lead us to pride in thinking we know and see more than others. Church history is littered with doctrinal disputes that can be illustrated by the analogy of how an elephant is understood by blind people; it all depends which part of the animal they are touching. Each part reveals a different truth, but they are all parts of the whole. As Paul stated: "*Now I know in part; then shall I know fully, even as I am fully known.*"[367]

When we attempt to judge others from our blindness, there is further consequence to our partial knowing. Apart from the revelation of the Spirit or a word of knowledge, we cannot fully know the heart or motive of anyone. In and of ourselves, we can only judge others from our own limited library of experience and knowledge … hence the caution "*Judge not, that ye be not judged.*"[368] Even Jesus said: "*But I pass no judgement without consulting the Father. I judge as I am told …*"[369] Even though He said that "*he knew what was in each person,*"[370] He still sought outside help from the Father. If Jesus didn't judge without His Father's help, how much less should we act as judge and jury over each other without divine revelation?

There are, of course, actions that are contrary to the Word of God that are open for judgement, but Isaiah states: "*Woe to those who are wise in their own eyes and clever*

---

364   Matthew 13:13 (NIV).

365   John 15:26 (KJV).

366   Psalm 32:8 (KJV).

367   1 Corinthians 13:12b (NIV).

368   Matthew 7:1 (KJV).

369   John 5:30a (TLB).

370   John 2:25b (NIV).

in their own sight.[371] God is the only one who is all seeing and all knowing; therefore, only He can judge justly.

Isaiah, Ezekiel, Daniel, and John clearly illustrate that even revelations of heavenly things have to be translated into images we can understand, as seen in the case of Elisha's servant: *"And Elisha prayed, 'Open his eyes, Lord, so that he may see.' Then the Lord opened the servant's eyes, and he looked and saw the hills full of horses and chariots of fire all around Elisha."*[372] When Christ was raised from the dead, He gave His disciples physical evidence—the black business card on the white fridge experience: *"Look at my hands! Look at my feet! You can see that it is I, myself! Touch me and make sure that I am not a ghost! For ghosts don't have bodies, as you see that I do!"*[373] Yet they were left unconvinced, still wondering, for it seemed "too good to be true."

Let us therefore learn the lessons from our blindness: *"If the blind lead the blind, both will fall into the pit."*[374] Open the eyes of my heart, Lord!

Shalom.

---

371   Isaiah 5:21 (NIV).

372   2 Kings 6:17 (NIV).

373   Luke 24:39 (NEI).

374   Matthew 15:14 (NIV).

59.
TAKING RISKS

As humans we live our lives in a tension between wanting the secure and predictable, and the desire to explore the unknown. We experiment with discovering, finding the new yet simultaneously needing the consistency of daily routine. It's the contrast between discovering the substance of the planet Jupiter and our daily visit to "Timmy's" for coffee; we need both experiences to satisfy our inner drives, but if one of these drives becomes stronger than the other, it creates imbalance. Humans need both—the predictable for the body, and the adventure and mystery for the soul. How do we fulfill these needs? We take risks—from those faltering first steps as an infant to placing those same feet on the moon later in life.

God has taken the biggest risk of all in making man in His own likeness and image.[375] While some theologians would disagree, as we review them we will discover just how much God risks (present tense) in all He has left up to His "kids." As parents we experience a similar pattern when faced with the independence of our children as they begin their own lives apart from us. Will they choose right and avoid sin and its consequences?

The Lord God placed the man in the garden as its gardener, to tend and care for it.

> But the Lord gave the man this warning: "You may eat of **any** fruit in the garden except fruit from the Tree of Conscience—for its fruit will open your eyes to make you aware of right and wrong, good and bad. If you eat its fruit, you will be doomed to die … And as they ate it, suddenly they became aware of their nakedness, and were embarrassed. So they strung fig leaves together to cover themselves around the hips.[376] (emphasis added)

God took a risk when He created beings with their own free will; that ability to choose meant they could of their own volition either return His love or decide not to. History proves the latter, but God's plan for man will not be frustrated. The

---

375 Genesis 1:26
376 Genesis 2:17; 3:7 (TLB).

vision of creatures created to be like God Himself is too incredibly wonderful for both the Creator and the created. Despite man's failure, God conceived a plan that would achieve His goal, and it would be even greater than if man had not failed. The question is … at what cost and risk?

This process has not been a "walk in the park" for either God or man. For His part, God had to risk that some of these created beings would choose Him while others would not, making the story laid out in the Bible simultaneously painful and glorious. The human drama had hardly started when one brother murdered another. Then as mankind multiplied, the whole risk venture began such a quick descent that scripture states: *"When the Lord God saw the extent of human wickedness, and that the trend and direction of man's lives were only towards evil, he was sorry he had made them. It broke his heart."*[377] Was the risk worth it, or did God risk too much?

Some parents fully identify with the pain God feels, while other couples who fear this potential suffering decide not to have children. The risk is too great because of what they have experienced in their own lives or seen in others. *God took the risk of creating man in His own image and likeness because He believed the risk was worth it.*

There are some successes but also lots of failures recorded in scripture. For every Enoch and Noah, there are not only King Sauls and Jeroboams, but also those He endorses with King David-like failures. God risked only because He thought it was worth it. The eleventh chapter of the book of Hebrews lists some of those for whom He thought it was "worth the risk."

Some believe that God has no emotions, but the Bible records both the joys and suffering He experiences. God is emotionally involved with His experiment of making beings like Himself. He states: *"Don't you think about what has happened to Judah and Jerusalem? I am as jealous as a husband for his captive wife."*[378] In another place He appeals: *"O Ephraim and Judah, what shall I do with you? For your love vanishes like morning clouds, and disappears like dew."*[379] Out of the cry of His heart He calls: *"I don't want your sacrifices—I want your love; I don't want your offerings—I want you to know me."*[380] He tells Judah *"… I wanted so much to bless you!"*[381] He appeals: *"I took care of you in the wilderness, in that dry and thirsty land. But when you had eaten and were satisfied, then you became proud and forgot me."*[382]

---

377   Genesis 6:5–6 (TLB).

378   Zechariah 1:14b (TLB).

379   Hosea 6:4 (TLB).

380   Hosea 6:6 (TLB).

381   Hosea 6:11b (TLB).

382   Hosea 13:5–6 (TLB).

God is torn like a lover who has been betrayed by his beloved, yet in looking at the journey from Adam to Israel: *"In all their distress he too was distressed ..."*[383] We must also consider the history of the church. God chose to "take the risk." It now becomes very personal; He has taken the risk with me, with my list of failures, but I am not alone. All of us belong to this family to some degree.

Some have criticized me for releasing certain people into places of ministry, but I am only following my Lord, who has released me ... and I know who I am. My cry is "not worthy," but He has taken the risk with me, and by God's grace, I am determined to see everyone who is part of this congregation released into God's destiny for their lives, whatever the risk. As I write this, I shed tears at God's amazing mercy and grace with me; He has "taken the risk."

One final note: Just as God had his King Sauls, I too have had mine. But just as this did not stop God, it will not stop me, because I believe we are *all worth the risk.*

Shalom.

---

383   Isaiah 63:9a (NIV).

60.
YOUR WILL VERSUS MY WILL

THE ELITE MORAL PUNDITS AND INTELLECTUALS OF OUR DAY HAVE DECIDED that a woman has complete control over her reproductive experience, giving her the right to abort any life conceived in the womb. Limitations have been placed around the timing, but these seem to be flexible enough to enable a woman who bore twins to try to abort one of them because she only wanted one child. The purpose of this article is not to debate the issue of abortion but the principle that allows an attitude permitting such heinous acts. Those who embrace abortion fly under the banner of MY CHOICE, and with the same agenda so do the LGBTQ (lesbian, gay, bisexual, transgender, and queer) community. I can and will be whatever sexual preference I CHOOSE, but it doesn't stop there. It's public knowledge that they would like to propose legislation permitting sex with minors, thinly disguised under the label "intergenerational sex." Under present law, this is a criminal offence, but considering the gains of the LBGTQ lobby in recent days, do not be surprised if this also becomes "normalized" in the same way their abduction of our educational system normalized previously unacceptable sexual behaviour.

The theme of today's life view is based on the principle of "my choice, my will be done," and it supersedes all historical moral and religious codes or laws. This new moral code ignores the lessons of history, along with its consequences, and instead blames those who object to the fruit of their own behaviour. Regrettably, mankind fails to realize that the pursuit of *my will* has its origin in the book of Genesis, when our first parents embarked on that fateful journey several millennia ago. Although deceived when they rebelled, the consequences have been catastrophic for the human race. God clearly expressed His will by telling them they could eat of any of the fruit of the trees in the Garden of Eden *except* the tree of the knowledge of good and evil.[384] It's no secret that the one advocating this disobedience was the original rebel himself, God's enemy, Satan. Humankind thinks they were choosing their own will ,when in fact it was actually Satan's.

Making decisions that ignore God's will bear fruit that is allied to Satan, not God—yes, even those kind acts that are rooted in rebellion against His will. As

---

384   Genesis 2:17.

Christians we may believe that this doesn't apply to us because we are "born again," but the battle still exists between God's will and ours, and doing our own thing produces terrible consequences: "Gay, bi-sexual men are more than seventeen times more likely to get anal cancer than other heterosexual men. In 2014, gay, and bisexual men who have sex with other men accounted for 83% of primary and secondary syphilis cases."[385]

Jesus nailed this issue in the prayer He taught His disciples: *your kingdom come, your will be done, on earth as it is in heaven.*[386] In His ministry He stated that He could only do what he saw the Father doing[387] and speak what the Father had taught Him.[388] In the Garden of Gethsemane when facing His role in bearing the total weight and consequences of all the sin of mankind, He prayed: *"Yet not what I will, but what you will."*[389]

Since we're being transformed into His image, why then should we consider that we can do our own thing, however good the act or motivation? There are only two wills we can choose: God's and our own. When we choose our own, we join Satan's rebellion.

The Christian doctrine of hell is the most difficult for many to reconcile: "All God does in the end with people is to give them what they want, including freedom from himself, what could be more fair than that?"[390] "There are only two kinds of people in the end: those who say to God, 'Thy will be done,' and those to whom God says, in the end, 'Thy will be done.' All that are in Hell choose it."[391] The journey to hell is a process that starts with being continually critical, judgemental, angry, bitter, unforgiving, self-centred, greedy, jealous, and lustful. It eventually ends with these patterns perpetuating and compounding themselves for eternity.

The good news is that God has made every provision to keep us from inheriting the fruit of our lives by taking the consequences on Himself—the innocent for the guilty. When Jesus was unjustly murdered on the cross, He achieved a reprieve for those who would repent, cease doing their own thing, and say, "Not my will, but Yours."

---

385 "Sexually Transmitted Diseases," *Centers for Disease Control and Prevention,* Accessed on June 1, 2018, https://www.cdc.gov/msmhealth/STD.htm.

386 Matthew 6:10 (NIV).

387 John 5:19.

388 John 8:28.

389 Mark 14:36b (NIV).

390 Timothy Keller, *The Reason for God,* (New York, NY: Penguin Group Inc., 2008), 82.

391 C.S. Lewis, *The Great Divorce,* (New York, NY: HarperCollins Publishers, 2001), 75.

This process doesn't end at that one decision but remains the root principle that guides our lives as Christians. The writer to the Hebrews gives us a serious caution: *"Never forget the warning, 'Today if you hear God's voice speaking to you, do not harden your hearts against him, as the people of Israel did when they rebelled against him in the desert.'"*[392] *"Since we have a kingdom nothing can destroy, let us please God by serving him with thankful hearts and with holy fear and awe. For our God is a consuming fire."*[393] Let us not continue to live according to *my will* and doing things that lead to hell. Scripture tells us: *"Mercy triumphs over judgement."*[394] When we repent and ask forgiveness, the eternal consequences of our rebellion are dealt with.

I have a personal, amplified version of the Lord's Prayer that I rehearse before God daily: *Your kingdom come in me, now, today; your will be done in me, now, today, just like it is in heaven and just like Jesus.* By the grace of God, empowered by the Holy Spirit, I endeavour to set my heart to live the Kingdom teaching of Jesus and to do the will of God.

Shalom.

392   Hebrews 3:15 (TLB).
393   Hebrews 12:28–29 (TLB).
394   James 2:13b (NIV).

61.
OFFENDED

THERE ARE SOME SITUATIONS IN LIFE THAT CUT US TO THE HEART SO DEEPLY, they can change our lives and impact not only who we are but also our eternal destiny. The harm they cause has the ability to destroy our relationship with God, ourselves, and each other unless we learn to recognize and deal with them. Unwittingly, we can become regular library visitors by continuously taking out books of offences, rehearsing and nursing them as though they were our children. The consequence is an established collection of hurts, with walls almost impenetrable by God or man.

Those who started following Jesus discovered that He was so controversial and unconventional, they continually had to re-evaluate their thinking about this "potential" Messiah. Their understanding of God's purposes for Israel and themselves was so challenged that many walked away from following Him.[395] They found His statements regarding drinking His blood and eating His flesh offensive,[396] and in the natural rightly so, but they failed to comprehend the spiritual nature of His words. Consequently, His words of life became words of death and wounded their religious life view, causing them to feed their offence with caustic comments about His family origins.[397] Jesus even challenged the twelve, asking if they wanted to leave Him too. Peter replied: "... to whom shall we go? You have the words of eternal life. We have come to believe and know you are the Holy One of God."[398]

We must embrace God's promise, given through the apostle Paul: "And we know that all things work together for good to them that love God, to them who are called according to his purpose."[399] If we fail to do this, we are no different today in our ability to grasp the spiritual issues behind every circumstance of life. Unless we see that even the wounds afflicted on us as part of God's plan for our benefit in the same way that Jesus was vilified, unjustly treated, and then murdered in public view, life will not make sense to us. The unjust death of Jesus achieved salvation for all mankind.

---

395   John 6:66.

396   John 6:53.

397   John 6:42.

398   John 6:68–69.

399   Romans 8:28 (KJV).

We will never know what is being accomplished in the heavenlies by the way we deal with our offences.

There is a terrible downside to reacting other than the way Jesus did when He called out from His agony: *"Father, forgive them, for the do not know what they are do-ing."*[400] Offences will not stay as a single wound, but will continue to "breed like rab-bits" until the offended becomes the offence itself, causing us to offend others with the same poison. The lesson? We can only share with others who we are as persons.[401]

One of the greatest challenges of life is admitting and confessing our failures, but we come by it honestly. Our first parents blamed others rather than admit their guilt,[402] and unless we recognize that harbouring offences is sin, we will never seek or find a solution for what ails us. The solution is to forgive those who have offended us,[403] and if Jesus could do that by forgiving those who crucified Him, then we must follow our leader and do the same. We are asked to forgive not only once, but seven-ty times seven times.[404] God has promised to give grace to those who do.

Now comes icing on the cake. We are also told to *"Bless them that curse you, and pray for them which despitefully use you."*[405] Although this process seems unnatural, this is the only way of cleansing the wounds inflicted on us so that we can be free. But there's more … there are two further steps we need to take to turn our forgive-ness into a lifestyle. The first is to give thanks *in* everything[406] followed by giving thanks *for* everything.[407] This is totally irrational to the natural man, but for those of us who are pursuing God's destiny for our lives, this makes eternal sense.

Once again, we are reminded:

*Moreover we know that to those who love God, who are called according to his plan, **everything** that happens fits into a pattern for good. God, in his fore-knowledge, chose them to bear the family likeness of his Son [conformed to the image], that he might be the eldest of a family of many brothers."*[408] (empha-sis added)

---

400 Luke 23:34a (NIV).
401 Hebrews 12:15.
402 Genesis 3:12.
403 Matthew 6:12.
404 Matthew 18:22.
405 Luke 6:28 (KJV).
406 1 Thessalonians 5:18.
407 Ephesians 5:20.
408 Romans 8:28–29 (PHILLIPS).

So be encouraged, because every offence we face has eternal benefits and is meant to help make us like Jesus.[409] What can be better than that?

> *And this I pray, that your love may abound still more and more in knowledge and all discernment, that you may approve the things that are excellent, that you may be sincere and without offense till the day of Christ, being filled with the fruits of righteousness which are by Jesus Christ, to the glory and praise of God.*[410]

Shalom.

---

409   2 Corinthians 6:4.

410   Philippians 1:9–11 (NKJV).

62.
SOMEONE HAS TO PAY

WHEN A CRIME IS COMMITTED, THERE ARE AT LEAST THREE PARTIES INVOLVED: the criminal, the victim, and the judicial system. If theft is the crime, then the victim may well lose all, but according to the Mosaic Covenant, the criminal had to repay five times the original value of the stolen object.[411] The only hope of the sentence being overturned was if the victim forgave the offence and bore the loss himself. In our present legal system, it's often the judge who decides what form of restitution (if any) should be paid. Since reimbursement is determined by the ability of the guilty party to pay, the innocent often bear the cost.

Jesus used a parable to illustrate the principles of forgiveness and the cost of the forgiving process. He said:

> *The Kingdom of heaven can be compared to a king who decided to bring his accounts up to date. In the process, one of his debtors was brought in who owed him $10 million … He couldn't pay, so the king ordered him sold for the debt, also his wife and children and everything he had. But the man fell down before the king, his face in the dust, and said, "Oh, sir, be patient with me and I will pay it all." Then the king was filled with pity for him and released him and forgave his debt. But when the man left the king he went to a man who owed him $2,000 … and grabbed him by the throat and demanded instant payment. The man fell down before him and begged him to give him a little time "Be patient and I will pay it," he pled. But his creditor wouldn't wait. He had the man arrested and jailed until the debt would be paid in full.*[412]

When the king discovers his behaviour, he states: "… *shouldn't you have mercy on others, just as I had mercy on you?*"[413]

Each of us has been forgiven by God for a debt we could not pay, yet He paid a debt He did not owe, and it cost Him everything to do it—the substitutionary death

---

411   Exodus 22:1
412   Matthew 18:23–30 (TLB).
413   Matthew 18:33 (TLB).

of His own Son. Because God is just, someone had to pay, and in our case, it was God Himself. But when we fail to forgive others, it annuls God's offer of forgiveness and we imprison ourselves because of the cost of our own debt. Mercy from God is dependent on our showing mercy to others.

Now for a reality check. Forgiveness isn't just a matter of saying "I forgive you." It cost the king $10,000,000. If the servant in the parable had mercifully forgiven the person, it would have cost him $2,000. The cost of forgiving others is equal to the degree of the sin committed against us, and we will need God's grace in order to be generous and merciful to others. Consequently, if we fail to forgive, God says He will not forgive us.[414]

Forgiveness may be easier said than done, particularly if the sin against you has deeply damaged your life, body, health, future, family, or home. The pain of it is further compounded by having to live with the tormenting memories of these events. Our natural desire is to want vengeance, but we are not to follow Clint Eastwood's pattern of a "go ahead, make my day" mentality. Instead, we are to submit to the scripture that states: *"Don't seek vengeance. Don't bear a grudge; but love your neighbor as yourself."*[415] This does not mean we do not seek justice, but that the chains of damage will cripple us for time and eternity unless we forgive from the heart.

Forgiveness has a price. The victim spirit can never be healed until forgiveness is freely given, and the cost of it is surrendering all claims for vengeance—whether or not justice is done. An attempt at justice was made when slavery was abolished in the British Empire in 1833. Slave owners had to be paid the full value of each slave, and it cost half the annual budget of the nation. Some called it "voluntary econocide." In the United States in 1865, the cost of liberating slaves equalled $4,000 for each person in today's currency.[416] Attempting to resolve issues legally does not touch the heart, which is why we still have grievance on both sides.

The final words in the parable quoted at the beginning state:

> *Then the man's [the one who owed $2,000] friends went to the king and told him what had happened. And the king called before him the man he had forgiven and said, "You evil hearted wretch! Here I forgave you all that tremendous debt, just because you asked me to—shouldn't you have mercy on others, just as I had mercy on you?" Then the angry king sent the man to the torture*

---

414 Matthew 6:14–15.

415 Leviticus 19:18 (TLB).

416 Timothy Keller, *The Reason for God* (New York: Riverhead Books, 2009), 65.

chamber until he had paid every last penny due. So shall my heavenly Father do to you if you refuse to truly forgive your brothers"[417]

Whatever it may cost us, let us freely forgive those who have sinned against us, because living a life of forgiveness is the only place of real freedom to love God and each other. Peter states:

Now you can have real love for everyone because your souls have been cleansed from selfishness and hatred when you trusted Christ to save you; so see to it that you really love each other warmly, with all your hearts.[418]

Shalom.

---

417   Matthew 18:31–35 (TLB).
418   1 Peter 1:22 (TLB).

63.
COLLATERAL DAMAGE

"SO SHALL MY FATHER DO TO YOU IF YOU REFUSE TO TRULY FORGIVE YOUR
brothers."[419] Some statements in scripture leave us without excuse or wiggle room
for doctrinal escapes in order to navigate a more convenient outcome. One such
portion is found in Paul's letter to the saints in Rome: "*For the wages of sin is death,
but the gift of God is eternal life in Christ Jesus our Lord.*"[420] He doesn't say that the
outcome of sin is just feeling guilty, sad, unhappy, or experiencing a loss of health,
friends, spouse, family, career, or even freedom. No, what he says is far worse—that
the consequence of sin is *death*, and while it may well include all of the above, the
final nail in the coffin is *eternal death*. Put bluntly, it's being separated from God
forever—but there is good news. We can exchange that *death* (sin's consequence)
for *eternal life* by accepting the substitutionary *death* of God's Son on our behalf, but
we can only receive it on the condition that we repent of our sin in order to obtain
the forgiveness God offers. There is, however, a warning attached to that condition.
If we do not forgive those who have sinned against us, that failure on our part annuls God's forgiveness toward us. You have to forgive your parents, children, family,
friends, enemies, employer, the government, the crazy driver, and, yes, even the dog!

Failure to forgive has collateral damage in every aspect of our lives, and regardless of what you may or may not believe about "eternal security," there are eternal
consequences. In the spiritual realm, unforgiveness not only gives Satan direct access to our hearts and minds, but harbouring it also impacts our mental health, causing us to make distorted and unwise decisions. Relationships become stunted, real
love is impossible to achieve, and it creates tension in family relationships, leaving
them shattered, maybe some even permanently.

You may well ask, "How can you make such a claim?" Proverbs tells us that:
"*Your own soul is nourished when you are kind; it is destroyed when you are cruel.*"[421]
Holding others to ransom and requiring vengeance is being cruel, especially when

---

419   Matthew 18:35 (TLB).

420   Romans 6:23 (NIV).

421   Proverbs 11:17 (TLB).

we expect mercy for ourselves. We think that time will heal, but unforgiveness "metastasizes" like cancer and infects every other part of our lives.

Our physical wellbeing is not immune either. Studies have demonstrated that there are many diseases, including cancer, that sometimes have their roots in unforgiveness. This isn't to say that the origin of all diseases is our sin, but sin was the first cause of all disease. As Christians, we are encouraged by James:

> Is anyone sick? He should call for the elders of the church and they should pray over him and pour a little oil upon him, calling on the Lord to heal him. And their prayer, if offered in faith, will heal him, for the Lord will make him well; and if his sickness was caused by some sin, the Lord will forgive him.[422]

John gives us the condition for receiving forgiveness: "*If we* **confess** *our sins, he is faithful and just and will forgive us our sins and purify us from all unrighteousness*"[423] (emphasis added). All Christians should be part of a congregation of believers. The New Testament has no other structure; one description of that relationship is "the body of Christ," showing that we are Christ's physical body on earth. Because we are a connected body, the action or non-action of one part affects the other parts; therefore, our failure to forgive does not stay with us but migrates to all members of the congregation, even if they aren't aware of our sin. Paul states the principle like this: "*If one part* [of the body] *suffers, all parts suffer with it, and if one part is honored, all the parts are glad.*"[424] Therefore, what happens in my life (whether I choose to forgive or not forgive) has a direct impact on the local assembly.

Unforgiveness has a ripple effect, like a stone thrown into a pool of water. Sin does not stop with the person involved but impacts first those who are closest, then the congregation, the region, county, province, nation, and eventually the world. But there is good news too. That same principle applies every time we bless others; when we are forgiving, kind, and loving, the results are impossible to contain. Proverbs tells us: "*Gentle words cause life and health; griping brings discouragement.*"[425]

Jesus shocked Peter when he told him how many times he should forgive, the number 470 was only an indication that there was no limit to forgiving, so stop counting! Forgiveness will unlock the mercy of God into all our lives so that as we pray for "the move of God," we step closer to the experience of the first century church:

---

422 James 5:14
423 1 John 1:9 (NIV).
424 1 Corinthians 12:26 (TLB).
425 Proverbs 15:4 (TLB).

And when the day of Pentecost was fully come [God's timing], they were all with one accord [unity] in one place [congregation of the saints]. And suddenly there came a sound from heaven as of a rushing mighty wind, and it filled all the house where they were sitting. And there appeared unto them cloven tongues like as of fire, and it sat on each of them."[426]

Although up to five hundred people had seen the resurrected Jesus on one occasion, only 120 filled the upper room. It doesn't take a multitude for God to pour out His Spirit. He has His people and His number with no gender, ethnic, or age limitations.

I believe the latter rain we are praying for will exceed what happened in Jerusalem and the first century church, but failure to forgive will lock us out of the next "move of God."

Shalom.

---

426   Acts 2:1–3 (KJV).

64.
PRIORITIES

BRENDA GAVE ME SOME SMALL FAMILY PICTURES AND ASKED ME TO TAKE THEM to the printers to get enlargements. I also have a generous list of people looking for my immediate input, as well as clients' expectations and church responsibilities, so which of the above should be my priority? I have to confess that I often do not set the right priorities, and Brenda has said that she sometimes feels like number ten on a list of five. There needs to be some repenting and change of behaviour on my part.

This may be a simple illustration, but it demonstrates a fundamental challenge we all face in choosing our priorities in the small and big things of life. What should be the ultimate main concern? Brenda feeling like number ten on my list of five tells me that my behaviour has relegated her to the bottom of the priority list. Still, life happens, and regardless of our relationship, sometimes life forces us to rearrange our priorities so that we can make short term decisions; this, however should be the exception, not the rule.

Continuous and repeated patterns expose a lack of true priority in the marriage relationship, or any other relationship for that matter. I realize that all relationships are complicated. We each have strengths and weaknesses, so how can we know what and when we should prioritize? The wisest man that ever lived said: *"But seek first his kingdom and his righteousness, and all these things will be given to you as well."*[427] This means more than our education, family, spouses, children, career, holidays, house, car, or grown up toys … including those addictive ones we make our main concern when we need a "fix." Unless we get the first one correct, all the others will claim first place in our hearts, minds, and pockets.

If you're still confused about your personal priorities, just check where you love to spend your money. Bingo! The answer is before you. But this isn't limited to the physical realm; any spiritual goals and ambitions not centred on God Himself become just as frustrating, because it's done in the flesh. We deceive ourselves, and that is the greatest deception of all. We were made for God Himself, and until we decide to put Him first, life will not have the correct priorities. Getting this straight

---

427   Matthew 6:33 (NIV).

is the only way we can correctly begin to sort out all the wants and claims and clear up the distractions.

We who are Spirit-filled Christians have God's promise of being "… *led by the Spirit of God are the sons of God*."[428] As we learn to obediently listen to His voice, He will enable us to set correct priorities so that we can say with Jesus: "*He does only what he sees the Father doing, and in the same way. For the Father loves the Son, and tells him everything he is doing*."[429] The two greatest commandments talk of loving God with "the works" (meaning with everything) and then loving each other with the same "works," because that's how He loves us.

Now back to the personal illustration. If I love Brenda with the "works," that should include her being my priority, and it should be my joy to go to the printers for her. When I consider how incredibly forgiving and patient God has been with me, I should be eager to love my wife by "doing acts of service," because that is just what God has done and continues to do for me. *My* attitude changes from being "self-centred" to "other centred." Some would appeal this claim, because our "self" would seem to disappear by always having others as our priority. This is the paradox found in the words of Jesus: "*Whoever finds their life will lose it, and whoever loses their life for my sake will find it*."[430] The more I die to self, the more I will live life and the more fully alive I become in Christ. This present society is totally bent out shape trying to "find themselves" when the answer is in the opposite direction.

If you think this option is foolishness, let me illustrate how we do this without any of the "God stuff." If you've ever experienced what we call "falling in love," then for a season your only desire is to love the other person by only wanting what pleases them. Once the chemical effects have worn off, you may well return to your self-centred life, but you cannot deny that you were so totally obsessed that you made that person your total priority. If you cannot identify or haven't experienced this form of relationship, then trust what millions of others say. Outside of the encounter with God, it is the most God-like experience you will ever have. I can't speak from experience, but I'm told that even the best "trip" drugs give you cannot compare with the God experience.

The incredibly good news is that making God your total and ultimate priority will open the door to a life more fulfilling than you could ever imagine. Your greatest pleasure will be in *loving, blessing, and serving God and others*, and that's where you'll find the real you, the one God created you to be.

---

428   Romans 8:14 (NIV).

429   John 5:19–20a (TLB).

430   Matthew 10:39 (NIV).

We sometimes don't realize that this is exactly what Jesus did:

Let your attitude to life be that of Christ Jesus himself. For he, who had always been God by nature, did not cling to his privileges as God's equal. But stripped himself of every advantage by consenting to be a slave by nature and being born a man. And plainly seen as a human being, he humbled himself by to a life of utter obedience, to the point of death, and the death he died was that of a common criminal. That is why God has now lifted him up to the heights, and has given him the name beyond all names, so that at the name of Jesus "every knee shall bow" whether in heaven or under the earth. And that is why "every tongue shall confess" that Jesus Christ is Lord to the glory of God he Father."[431]

The path down to humility is the only path up.
Shalom.

---

431   J.D. Phillips, *The New Testament in Modern English*, rev. (New York: Simon and Schuster, 1995), Philippians 2:6–11).

65.
HELP LINE?

Recently, Bell deleted the ability of my cell phone to receive emails, which has caused some serious inconvenience. I have spent hours on the phone with Central America, India, the Philippines, and once in Canada trying to get this service restored but to no avail; four visits to the Bell store in the mall didn't help either. I watched a CBC *Marketplace* documentary dealing with this problem, only to discover that all the obstructions and hours on the phone is a deliberate policy of all three phone companies to make you stop bothering their "help line." I can't afford any more hours, so the strategy has worked with me. It's evident that there is no way to "go to the top" to get answers in this bureaucratic system.

This is a perfect example of the attitude of the kingdom of this world. While "going to the top" for an answer is not an option on this planet, in God's kingdom we have direct access to Him, all because of what Jesus has done. He taught us to address God as "Our Father," and it doesn't get much better than that for "going to the top." For some reason, human nature is never satisfied with such a simple solution. Some have complicated it by introducing Mary, the saints, and priests, and then a bureaucracy that has placed a wedge between God and us. It cost God's Son His life in order to rip the veil in the Holy of Holies from top to bottom.[432] What an insult to Christ's work of grace for direct access!

God doesn't put us on hold. We believers don't have to listen to the same old music interposed periodically with the lie "your call is important to us," because Jesus, our "middle man," has cleared the way for us to go directly to the top: "*So let us come boldly to the very throne of God and stay there to receive his mercy and find grace to help us in our times of need.*"[433] As one TV commercial puts it: we don't have to be "pushed around by the big phone companies." We go straight to the top, God Himself where there are no hour-long waits, because the line is open 24/7. We're even told that God's Son can fully sympathise with our weaknesses, as "*he himself has shared fully in all our experience of temptation, except that he never sinned.*"[434]

---

432 Matthew 27:51.

433 Hebrews 4:16 (TLB).

434 Hebrews 4:15b (PHILLIPS).

Jesus has paid it fully, and we get complete access to all channels. There are no additional costs in this contract, but there are conditions: *"If you remain in me and my words remain in you, ask whatever you wish, and it will be done for you."*[435] He added: *"Ask and it will be given to you [whatever you ask for], seek and you will find; knock and the door will be opened to you."*[436] The Message version states it like this; *"Be direct. Ask for what you need. This isn't a cat-and-mouse, hide-and-seek game we're in* [like the phone companies]. *If your child asks for bread, do you trick him with sawdust?"*

God has our eternal welfare at heart. There are some prayers He refrains from answering because He doesn't want what happened to the children of Israel to happen to us. He gave them what they wanted, but it sent leanness to their souls.[437]

There are times God wants to develop perseverance in our relationship with Him so that we will be encouraged to always pray and never give up, because *"God will surely give justice to his people who plead with him day and night. He will answer them quickly!"*[438] Definitely not like the phone companies! Yet at other times we will be required to freely forgive, just as we have been freely forgiven.[439]

Similar to our battles with phone companies is the cosmic war going on, which is more real than flesh and blood. Paul tells us that we need protective armour, of which prayer in the Spirit is a vital part. He tells the Ephesian Christians: *"For our fight is not against any physical enemy … We are up against the unseen power that controls this dark world, and spiritual agents from the very headquarters of evil."*[440]

When we see the "help line" become the "hindrance line" at the phone companies, we are seeing a reflection of the moral code of this dark world. Every endeavour of man, however noble in its idealism, will in some way mirror this pattern. If not initially, then eventually all their good endeavours will be consumed by those dark forces. You don't require a university degree to see the corruption in government, car companies, education, and even health care with pharmaceutical companies pushing excessive medication: "… statistics clearly show that for the first time ever in the U.S.A. prescription drugs have killed more people than car accidents …"[441]

---

435   John 15:7 (NIV).

436   Matthew 7:7 (NIV).

437   Psalm 106:15.

438   Luke 18:7–8a (TLB).

439   Matthew 18:23–24.

440   Ephesians 6:12 (PHILLIPS).

441   Vivian Goldschmidt, "New Report: More Deaths Caused by Prescription Drugs than by Car Accidents," *Saveinstitute,* Accessed on June 1, 2018, https://saveourbones.com/more-deaths-caused-by-prescription-drugs-than-by-car-accidents/.

There are only two kingdoms, and Jesus said that we can't serve one without hating the other: "*No one can serve two masters; for either he will hate the one and love the other, or else he will be loyal to the one and despise the other. You cannot serve God and mammon.*"[442] Before we were saved we were part of that other kingdom, even though we didn't know it. It's even more important now that we belong to God's kingdom that we take up arms against the enemy of all that is good and of God. Our prayers are an important part of God's method of dealing with the hordes of Satan, so let us continually "go direct" to our God and pray for all men everywhere at all times.

Shalom.

---

442   Matthew 6:24 (NKJV).

66.
THE SIMPLE THINGS

WE LIVE IN A WORLD THAT IS GROWING INCREASINGLY COMPLEX—TO SUCH AN
extent that we are prone to miss the simple things of life. We have more technology
and accumulated knowledge than we have brain matter to handle it, and this has
caused us to lose our appreciation for the fundamentals of life.

Some years ago, I picked up a small book entitled *Practicing His Presence*. It
consisted mostly of the short diary notes of two men who lived some three hundred
years apart. I had never before read a book illustrating the most uncomplicated relationship with God that these two men described. Observing their experience of intimacy with God stirred up a deep hunger in me for the same type of relationship. I
asked God if this simple yet profound experience was possible for a normal married
man with a wife, three kids, a full time professional career that demanded regular
international travel, and a commitment to leadership to this local church. Saying my
life was "full" in the sense that every moment seemed to have claims on it was not an
exaggeration. As I have previously confessed, Brenda has sometimes said she feels
like number ten on a list of five.

I took up the challenge of pursuing an uncomplicated, intimate relationship
with God, and I readily confess to more failures than successes. I am now, however,
more determined than ever to follow the path these men took. I realized from the
outset that it not only requires God's grace, but also my commitment to follow not
just their steps but those of Christ Himself, who said; "... *The Son can do nothing by
himself. He does only what he sees the Father doing, and in the same way. For the Father
loves the Son, and tells him everything he is doing* ..."[443]

I can pray, study the Word, attend a multitude of meetings, do acts of kindness
and love, counsel, help, teach, preach, save souls, heal the sick, cast out demons, be
part of leadership in a congregation, and even become my own Wikipedia—and on
and on and on. But let's not forget the words of Jesus: "... *I never knew you: depart from
me, ye that work iniquity*."[444] How easily one could say that of my life. The simple thing
that He wants from us is to know us and for us to know Him. Now how complicated

---

443   John 5:19 20a (TLB).
444   Matthew 7:23b (KJV).

is that? My experience, however, has taught me that *the most simple is the most difficult.* Regardless of the life we face, intimacy with God is priority number one. Though I have covered this topic in a previous article, I still find it the most challenging.

I re-read the book and realized that it doesn't require a university degree, seminary or Bible college training, or even being clever … in fact, all of these can sometimes be more of a hindrance than a help. As Jesus set a child in their midst, He said: *"… I say unto you, Whosoever shall not receive the kingdom of God as a little child shall in no wise enter therein."*[445] One man in the book was a seminary graduate and a missionary, while the other a monk in a monastery, but neither man found the sort of intimate relationship with God their hearts craved in a place or a ministry.

I have previously shared how I pursued Brenda till I won her hand in marriage, but that was only the first step; the real challenge was to discover her heart. All my past love letters and even my present efforts are empty unless I engage her heart. So it is with God, but the good news is that He has been seeking me all along and has cleared every possible obstacle out of the way so that we can enjoy each other.

Some may say: "Well, what about the great commission?" Let me tell you that I love to do things for Brenda because I love her—not to make her love me. Our motive to serve comes out of the intimacy of love; any other way cheapens the relationship. I don't give to get. I give because I love, and it doesn't get much better than that! God has already set the pattern by giving so hugely, and we can never measure the degree of what He has given. They say it takes two to tango, and God will lead if we will desire to follow in His dance steps and choose to walk in the rhythm of His Holy Spirit!

God has clearly demonstrated that He desires an intimate relationship with us, and according to the Apostle John's description, *"God is love."*[446] In other words, the very essence of God is love. Just in case you think I'm becoming too mystical, let me remind you that when the triune God (Elohim) made us like Himself, He reproduced this incredible relationship with man. To ensure there's no misunderstanding, *triune* doesn't mean that there are three Gods, but that there are three persons forming one God.

We see the same pattern in the creation of woman. God took Eve out of man to be his helpmate, and then God told them to become one again. The intimacy that the triune God enjoys is the pattern He has set for husband and wife, but we all know how this simple plan is so difficult to achieve, and we all know it's so difficult because the introduction of the sin nature caused us to turn from being other-centred to

---

445   Luke 18:17 (KJV).

446   1 John 4:8.

being self-centred. Still, we all have this deep knowing that there must be more; hence, we try again and again with multiple attempts, like Solomon with seven hundred wives and three hundred concubines.

Let me close with a few tempting quotes from one of the men in the book:

This year I have started out to live all my waking moments in conscious listening to the inner voice, asking without ceasing 'What, Father, do you desire this minute?' It is clear that this is exactly what Jesus was doing all day every day.[447]

I have tasted a thrill in fellowship with God which has made anything discordant with God disgusting.[448]

I have found such a way of life. I ask nobody else to live it, or even try it. I only witness that it is wonderful, it is indeed heaven on earth. And it is *very simple, so simple that any child could practice it*" (emphasis added).[449]

Oh, if we only let God have His full chance He will break our heart with the glory of His revelation. It is my business to look into the very face of God until I ache with bliss.[450]

Shalom.

---

447 Brother Lawrence (Nicolas Herman in Hériménil) and Frank Laubach, *Practicing His Presence* second printing (Goleta, CA: Christian Books, 1976), 2.

448 Ibid., 13.

449 Ibid., 26.

450 Ibid., 23.

67.
SUSTAINABLE REVIVAL

THE WORLD IS FINALLY DISCOVERING THAT GREEDILY RAPING THE PLANET IS the road to extinction, and now almost everything must be "sustainable." A group of us at F.C.C. spent several weeks studying Rick Joyner's book, *World Aflame*, chapter by chapter, and then praying into those situations with the anticipation of experiencing a similar move. The book covers the Welsh Revival of 1904. The fact that the book only covers one year leads to a searching question: What happened in 1905? Joyner deals with this issue at some length, searching for reasons as to why the actual outward manifestation appeared to last only ten months.

Objectively one can say that the fruit has lasted up to this day. The revival has impacted the worldwide Pentecostal movement, of which three were in the U.K.: the Elim Church, the Assemblies of God, and the Apostolic Church (which is our affiliation in Canada). But the question teasing me is: How much bigger could it have been if it was sustainable?

The book documents that within those ten months, Christians became totally committed to God. Prayer meetings were full from morning to night, with those praying breaking into "singing in the Spirit." There were over 100,000 saved. There were empty pubs, unemployed police, vacant sports arenas, packed churches and chapels, and miners singing songs of worship and praise as they cut seams of coal. So why wasn't it sustained?

Joyner offers some answers, and I have lived long enough to experience the Jesus People movement of the early 1970s, the charismatic movement, the Catacombs youth revival of Toronto, the "New Wine" movement, and the Toronto Blessing and its sister move in Brownsville, Florida, but none of them have been sustainable in their original vigour and passion. As was demonstrated in Brownsville, from a purely physical standpoint, the time and emotional demands are unsustainable, but I do see a way of maintaining every level of our encounter with God.

From my own experience, I can see that each revival/renewal has deepened my experience and relationship with God. It has continued to reveal the purpose of why He said: "*Let us make mankind in our image, in our likeness …*"[451] I have retained some

---

451   Genesis 1:26a (NIV).

of the fruit from each of these "moves of God," which has created in me a desire for more of the knowledge and experience of God and His purposes. The danger in each of these revival experiences is that we only retain the outward manifestations and rituals rather than the work of the Spirit. I've heard it said that the only thing that remains when the dove has gone is the dung.

Jesus prayed that we would become one with God just like He was, and I see this as the ultimate goal of the redemptive process. Becoming "one with each other" as part of the body of Christ, or in marriage, requires that both parties die to a self-centred walk, and so it is that, *"... that all of them may be one, Father ... I in them and you in me."*[452] God's part has been done in Christ in order to *"reconcile all things to Himself,"*[453] but God's work requires something of us. If this oneness is to take place, He commands us to die to ourselves. This is how love works, and it is the ultimate sustainable encounter. God proved His love by dying on our behalf so that we could respond to His love, but there's a cost to pay in order to become one in love with Him— we must habitually die to ourselves.

This is the technical explanation, but how does it work in practice? This is where my earlier article, "The Simple Things," applies. The experience of knowing someone can lead to loving them; likewise, loving someone can lead to knowing them. As for our relationship with God, He has revealed His love for us, and He knows us like no other because He knew us even before we were born. The challenge lies at our end, and the solution is spending time with Him. But you may say, "I can't join a monastery." The good news is you don't have to— just develop the habit of sharing everything you do and say with Him no matter how small or insignificant it might seem.

It's my understanding that we all talk to ourselves to one degree or another, so why not change the direction of our "conversation" and talk to God instead? If we do this habitually, we'll find that we have brought God into our every moment. He said: "... [He] *will rejoice over you with singing."*[454] Jesus said that He wants us to be one, as He and the Father are one.

As previously stated, the ultimate goal of the redemptive process is to become one with God. It's the only way to fulfil the original plan of being mankind in his image and likeness so that we can enjoy each other forever. This is sustainable because we can learn to do this all day long, no matter where we go. God has given us His Holy Spirit to be our teacher, our prompter, and our power to enable Him to form

---

452   John 17:21, 23 (NIV).

453   Colossians 1:20

454   Zephaniah 3:17 (NIV).

God's character in us. "God is love," which means that being one with Him is totally sustainable, but only because it's Him doing the sustaining. He will enable us to be just as Jesus was when He lived amongst us in the flesh: "*I and the Father are one.*"[455]

Let your employment be to know God. The more you actually know him the more you will desire to know him. Since knowledge is a measurement of love, the deeper and more intimate you are with Him, the greater will be your love for him.[456]

Shalom.

---

455 John 10:30 (TLB).

456 Brother Lawrence (Nicolas Herman in Hériménil) and Frank Laubach, *Practicing His Presence*, second printing (Goleta, California: Christian Books, 1976), 105.

68.
KNOW YOUR ENEMY

It's an interesting observation that most of our relationships are either about controlling or being controlled. Let me explain. The recent death of Fidel Castro provoked reviews of his legacy, and despite the naive view of Justin Trudeau, consensus is that he was a cruel, dominating, controlling dictator of Cuba. Having visited Cuba many times on business, I became privy to the Cuban experience of the extent of that control, such as the closure and padlocking of all churches as well as governmental control of all schools and businesses. There was no freedom of speech, nor was there any distinction in pay levels. Payment for all doctors, surgeons, electricians, and teachers came to the equivalent of twenty US dollars per month. It was total control of every Cuban in every aspect of their lives.

North Korea, the old Soviet Union, and the past Nazi regime of Germany exercised complete domination over their populations. We face a similar challenge in the Western so-called free democracies. Even Justin Trudeau demands everyone in the Liberal caucus to vote "pro-choice" relative to women's rights, regardless of the individual's beliefs or moral code; it's an echo of the first century church being compelled to affirm that "Caesar is Lord." Back then you could have any and as many gods as you liked, but Caesar trumped them all. Failure to accept his divinity brought the entire weight of the Roman system against you. Political correctness has hindered our freedom of speech to the degree that we can no longer safely speak the truth openly without the threat of legal retribution.

Another glaring example of this are the quasi-scientists who control the teaching in all levels of our educational system by imposing the theory of evolution while prohibiting the teaching of any creation views. Then there is the LGBTQ community that has a stranglehold on everything relative to expressions of sexuality. They are not interested in reality. Their goal is to control those with opposite views in order to normalize deviant sexual behaviour. And let's not forget the globalization of business in order to create monopolies of power.

Wherever you look you'll find domination. Sad to say, with its history of inquisitions, burnings at the stake, and ethnic and religious cleansings, the church is not immune. It's evident that a "spirit of control" can even motivate individual Christians. Who, or what, is behind this desire to control everything and everyone?

Denominations control their followers, clergy control the laity, church boards control pastors, and men, women, spouses each other and their children.

Matthew's Gospel describes how Satan tempted Jesus with the option to achieve control of the kingdoms of the world:

> ... the devil took him to a very high mountain, and from there showed him all the kingdoms of the world and their magnificence. "Everything there I will give you," he said to him, "if you will fall down and worship me."[457]

This temptation reveals, amongst other things, that the kingdoms of this world belong to the devil, because Jesus never challenged him but replied: "*Away with you, Satan ... the scripture says, 'You shall worship the Lord your God, and him only shall you serve.'*"[458] There are only two kingdoms. Satan's is ruled by the "spirit of control," and God's by the "spirit of freedom." They are two diametrically opposing kingdoms. This religious spirit is opposite to the Spirit of God, as Jesus said to the teachers of the Law:

> For you are the children of your father the devil and you love to do the evil things he does. He was a murderer from the beginning and a hater of truth—there is not an iota of truth in him. When he lies, it is perfectly normal; for he is the father of liars.[459]

Similarly, "Islam" means "submission," and when applied means control over every aspect of life.

When Jesus' disciples asked Him how to pray, He included this statement: "*Your kingdom come now, your will be done now on earth as in heaven.*"[460] One of the most obvious fruits of Satan's kingdom is the "spirit of control," and it manifests itself in all sorts of expressions in the church. I recall that during the charismatic renewal of the 1970s there was a need to disciple Christians from denominations that had not previously experienced the baptism of the Holy Spirit. Leaders promoted a teaching entitled "The Discipleship Movement," but that too became a controlling spirit. In the name of discipline, elders and leaders ended up controlling every aspect

---

457   Matthew 4:8–9 (PHILLIPS).
458   Matthew 4:10 (PHILLIPS).
459   John 8:44.
460   Matthew 6:10 (ONMB).

of Christians' lives—to the degree that they needed input before buying a fridge. It was exposed and repented of, but it does show how easily the other kingdom can invade God's. We would do well to remember that we reproduce after our own kind.[461]

When we see the spirit of control manifest in the church, it's always in conflict with the Kingdom of God. Man's ideas are not God's, and because of the fall, Satan rules man's kingdoms. *"For my thoughts are not your thoughts, neither are your ways my ways, saith the Lord. For as the heavens are higher than the earth, so are my ways higher than your ways, and my thoughts than your thoughts."*[462]

Here then is the caution: even *all our good ideas* can come from the *other* kingdom. We must learn to discern God's thoughts and strategy in all that we do, because *"... anyone who chooses to be a friend of the world* [the *other* kingdom] *becomes an enemy of God ... Submit yourselves, then, to God* [His kingdom]. *Resist the devil* [the *other* kingdom], *and he will flee from you."*[463]

Shalom.

---

461   Genesis 1:11.

462   Isaiah 55:8–9 (KJV).

463   James 4:4, 7.

69.
SON OF GOD AND SON OF MAN

FROM THE MOMENT OF ITS CONCEPTION, MANY HAVE CHALLENGED THE CHURCH regarding the person and work of Christ. The first three centuries were torn with various doctrines concerning the divinity and manhood of Christ to such a degree that it provoked church leaders to gather in Nicaea in 325 BC (now in Islamic Turkey) to draft the Nicene Creed. It states in part: "We believe in one God the Father almighty, Maker of heaven and earth, of all things visible and invisible. And in one Lord Jesus Christ, the only-begotten Son of God, begotten of the Father before all worlds." The Definition of Chalcedon of 451 AD developed it even further: "… we all with one accord teach men to acknowledge one and the same Son, our Lord Jesus Christ, at once complete in the Godhead and complete in manhood, truly God and truly man …" While genuine mainstream Christianity accepts that Jesus is fully God and fully man, there are various cults, such as the Mormons and Jehovah Witnesses, that have doctrines about Jesus ascribing Him less than "*the Word was made flesh*."[464]

While this somewhat theological introduction is a departure from my usual one, I'm hoping it won't turn you off but will instead persuade you to hear me out. My purpose is show you some very exciting things about the way Jesus lived and how it applies to us today. The Son of God became a man to enable men to become sons of God. Whenever we talk of the person, position, life, teaching, and work of salvation of Jesus Christ, we must be sure that we understand that He is both fully God and fully man. Paul tells us what the end game is. We are to be "*conformed to the image of his Son*"[465] But how can sinners like us become like Christ? The plan was for Christ to become a man so that He could experience all the tests and temptations we face but not sin in the process. Paul says it this way:

> For he, who had always been God by nature, did not cling to his prerogative as God's equal, but stripped himself of all privilege by consenting to be a slave by nature and being born as a mortal man. He humbled Himself by living a life

---

464   John 1:14 (KJV).
465   Romans 8:29 (KJV).

of utter obedience, even to the extent of dying, and the death he died was that of a common criminal."[466]

Jesus described His life on earth as one of total submission to the Father: "... *the Son can do nothing by himself; he can only do what he sees the Father doing, because whatever the Father does the Son also does.*"[467] He then informed His disciples that they were in the same position: "... *apart from me you can do nothing.*"[468] Jesus limited Himself as "Son of Man." He so depended on the Father and the Holy Spirit to enable Him to do the works of the kingdom that He didn't even commence His ministry until He was filled with the Holy Spirit. Since Jesus is our "prototype," we are to follow that same pattern and process so that we may become "sons of God: "... *God sent his Son, born of a woman, born under law, to redeem those under the law, that we might receive adoption to sonship,*"[469] doing even "*greater things than these.*"[470]

The thrilling hope we have in choosing to follow the exact steps of Christ is that we will become "Christ" to the world. I can hear the objections to this claim as we look at the reality of our own lives and the church in general, but Jesus would not have made these statements unless they were possible. I want to avoid making excuses for myself or the universal church by interpreting His words as meaning less than their face value, because He clearly states: "... *and these signs will accompany those who believe ...*"[471]

As Son of Man, Jesus can empathize with us:

For we do not have a high priest who is unable to empathize with our weaknesses, but we have one who has been tempted in every way, just as we are— yet without sin. Let us then approach God's throne of grace with confidence, so that we may receive mercy and find grace to help us in our time of need.[472]

I want show you that as the Son of Man, Jesus lived His life on earth the same way we are to live ours. Although this doesn't diminish His identity as the Son of God, it does raise our vision to see the possibility of being like Him—but there is

---

466   Phillipians 2:6–8 (PHILLIPS).
467   John 5:19 (NIV).
468   John 15:5b (NIV).
469   Galatians 4:4–5 (NIV).
470   John 14:12 (NIV).
471   Mark 16:17 (NIV).
472   Hebrews 4:15–17 (NIV).

a difference. While we acknowledge that Jesus was sinless from conception by the Holy Spirit, we also admit that we are the opposite in that we were conceived in sin; "… *and in sin did my mother conceive me*.[473] But this is the miracle—He fulfilled His promise by giving us the Holy Spirit so that by character and gifting we might live and do the same works. Regrettably, the church has placed such a vast chasm between what Jesus was and did that we make Him so other-worldly we cannot conceive becoming "conformed to the image of his Son." I know I quote this a lot, but I believe it's worth repeating His own prayer for His disciples: "*that all of them may be one, Father, just as you are in me and I am in you*."[474] Let's not forget that He also said that they would do even greater things than He did. The first century church did just that: "*Then the disciples went out and preached everywhere, and the Lord worked with them and confirmed his word by the signs that accompanied it*."[475] Scripture even states that from Paul's hands many miracles were done: "*God did extraordinary miracles through Paul*."[476]

We the church, "the called-out ones," are both individually and collectively "Christ" on earth. Paul describes us as the "body of Christ" and he instructs us to do what he did, even to the forgiving of sins when people repent. We may be allergic to this command because of the abuse of the "confessional," but these are still his instructions. He also portrays us as an army and tells us that we do not battle against people, "*but against principalities, against powers*."[477] We are not only to take on these mighty spiritual beings in prayer and bring them under our feet, but we are also to heal the sick, raise the dead, cast out demons, and preach the good news to all nations with the same power of the Holy Spirit as Jesus had. Jesus did not command us to make only converts or followers. No, our command is to make disciples ("Christs" meaning to become like Christ) of all nations.

We are part of a wonderful plan of the restoration of all things. We are not passive observers but vital, active partners with God, and by the power of the Holy Spirit, we do the same as *Jesus* did when He validated the word He spoke through His mighty works and miracles.

Shalom.

---

473   Psalm 51:5b (KJV).

474   John 17:21a (NIV).

475   Mark 16:20 (NIV).

476   Acts 19:11 (NIV).

477   Ephesians 6:12 (KJV).

70.
GRAFFITI

Graffiti: from the Italian to mean "scratched" into stone, as in prison walls.

BRENDA AND I RECENTLY SPENT SIX DAYS VISITING SOME WESTERN EUROPEAN cities in France, Italy, Sicily, Malta, and Spain. All of them had a two thousand year plus historical heritage, but long heritage wasn't the only thing they shared. The one dominant thing they all had in common (and no, it was not the architecture or church buildings) was graffiti. Every available wall, store, and monument was desecrated by spray paint, and it appeared that no one had any interest in attempting to remove or cover its crudeness. This age and generation has birthed a total disrespect for any heritage of our Christian culture, and graffiti is but one outward expression of that contempt.

Homo sapiens have a destructive penchant for marring all that is good and then having the audacity to call it art, but their re-labelling perverts natural morality by redefining it as "approved behaviour." What's behind this human activity and desire to foul everything beautiful? Could it be the "Destroyer" of Revelation 9:11 himself, whose agenda is to attack everything that is good and beautiful, whether part of creation, works of beauty (especially man), or God's masterpiece of creation?

God created the heavens and the earth and placed our original forefathers in a beautiful garden. There was harmony between man, animals, vegetation, and God until one day a spoiler came to deceive Eve into believing that God was withholding the most important thing of all—the ability to be like God.[478] By choosing to believe the words of the "deceiver," they disobeyed God's order, and the rest, as they say, is history. Graffiti was born out of the root of rebellion, along with every other curse the world has endured since the fall. Man has raped the planet in his greed by not following the instructions as God's representative to subdue it, take charge of it, and have dominion over it. When man made that decision, he separated himself from God and infected his soul with a destructive sin nature that caused him to reproduce the character of the "destroyer" himself. The fact that every brilliant invention can be turned into a tool for evil is evidence enough of this perverse human bent, and all because man has made himself a self- centered "god" rather than a "Creator-God" centred man. Despite this perversion, the memory of the God-nature in man still strives to create beauty and order.

The Christian message contains the plan for the total restoration of man to a level beyond that state of Genesis innocence, but it cost the Creator "Himself" an investment that we will never be able to fully comprehend. This restoration includes the natural world. The Apostle John describes it this way: *"Then I saw a new sky and a new earth, for he first sky and first land passed away, fading from sight."*[479]

Years before John's revelation, the Apostle Paul saw and wrote:

> *The whole creation is on tiptoe to see the wonderful sight of the sons of God coming into their own. The world of creation cannot as yet see reality, not because it chooses to be blind, but because in God's purpose it has been so limited—yet it has been given hope. And the hope is that in the end the whole of created life will be rescued from the tyranny of change and decay, and have its share in that magnificent liberty which can only belong to the children of God!*[480]

It's plain to anyone with eyes to see that at the present time all created life groans in a sort of universal travail.

The root problem we face is that we are fallen creatures living in a fallen world, and our hope is not found with the environmentalists and their message to save the planet. As Christians, we need to continue following the original mandate relative to every aspect of life. As God's stewards, it's our responsibility "to take care of it" while at the same time pray *"your kingdom come, your will be done, on earth as it is in heaven"*[481] until "the new heavens and new earth" come, as described by John: *"And then the devil, who deceived them, was thrown violently into the lake of burning sulfur, where the beast and the false prophet had been thrown. They will be tormented day and night forever and ever."*[482]

God will deal with our mutual enemy and He will complete His masterpiece of the restoration project in man.

> *Then I heard a loud voice from the throne saying, "Behold the dwelling of God is with mankind and they will be his people"… And he will wipe away every*

---

479   Revelation 21:1 (OMB).

480   Romans 8:19–21 (PHILLIPS).

481   Matthew 6:10 (NIV).

482   Revelation 21:3–5 (NIV).

*tear from their eyes and death will no longer be, there will neither mourning nor crying or pain because the first things went away. Then the one who sits on the throne said "**Behold, I make all things new.**"*[483] (emphasis added)

We have a hope and a future that those who do not trust Him cannot understand. Even as we see how mankind pollutes God's earth, we look forward to the restoration of all things.

Shalom.

P.S. As an Interior Designer, I have a desire to reflect God's creative spirit by endeavouring to create beautiful spaces for humans to enjoy.

---

483 Revelation 21:3–5 (OMNB).

71.
THE ORIGIN OF LOVE

THERE IS AN OLD ADAGE THAT SAYS, "LOVE MAKES THE WORLD GO ROUND." Evolutionary biologists believe it's just chemical reactions between people or things, but song writers, singers, and musicians thrive on it. Poets write words about it that read like music, and the retail world adores Valentine's Day because it's the second-best selling season of the year. Jewellery shops would close without it, and all of us have experienced it in one form or another, whether it's love for your favourite pet, car, holiday, hobby, first boy or girlfriend, spouse, house, or whatever you care to name. At its fundamental root, it is our personal engagement and attachment to people or things that evokes pleasure in us. The force of that feeling can be so powerful that we are sometimes even prepared to die for it. Love can't be measured; we can only experience it, and it begs the question: Where did this incredibly powerful and motivating force come from? It is only the most foolish who attribute it purely to a chemical reaction, as that is only a consequence, not the cause.

"I have an itch; therefore, I scratch," says the old proverb. Every appetite tells us that there must be a way of satisfying that desire; there must be an origin. The very structure of the natural world confirms our assumption that an appetite for food means that food exists to satisfy our hunger. We have this innate desire to give and receive love; therefore, its origin must be outside of ourselves and cannot be answered by any evolutionary theory. The Apostle John tells us that *"God is love,"*[484] and in his book, *Mere Christianity*, C.S. Lewis explains that "God is love" and has no real meaning unless God contains at least two persons.[485] The reality is that love, by its very nature, endorses our belief and understanding of the Trinity. Genesis explains man's creation like this: *"We will make mankind in our image and after our likeness."*[486] In the ONMB version, the word "we" is the plural Hebrew name of God, "Elohim," which translated means "Gods." It is therefore evident that the triune God has always experienced a relationship of love. Consequently, it's clear that love has its origin in the triune God.

---

484   1 John 4:16 (NIV).

485   C.S. Lewis, *Mere Christianity* (San Francisco, CA: HarperCollins, 1952), 174–176.

486   Genesis 1:26 (ONMB).

God fashioned the creative process to repeat the likeness and image of "Elohim;" hence, we are designed to love. God made us to both need and give love. He does not need love, but He has chosen to desire our love, just as parents enjoy and desire their children's love. Studies have shown that physical touch and love are so important, babies who do not receive any affection are more prone to die prematurely than those who do; in fact, even a rejected and unwanted child in the womb is susceptible to being emotionally maimed.

God *is* love. That's the very essence of His nature, and since we were made in His likeness and image, we were also created to love and be loved. Consequently, love is our first and primary motivation. We see in the working of the Trinity that the Son submits in love to the Father: "... *yet not my will, but yours be done.*"[487] The Father loves and endorses the Son: "*You are my Son, whom I love; with you I am well pleased.*"[488] Then there's the Spirit, who reveals the Son and teaches us about Him: "*But when the Father sends the Comforter instead of me—and by the Comforter I mean the Holy Spirit—he will teach you much, as well as remind you of everything I myself have told you.*"[489]

This Triune pattern of the relationship between the Father, Son, and Holy Spirit is reflected in our own nature in that we are spirit, soul, and body, and even these can be sub-divided into three parts; for example, the soul is composed of mind, will, and emotions. This is important for us to understand, because as "fallen" creatures, every part of our nature has been disconnected. I can hear some saying, "But there are more meanings to "love" than just the English word *love*." I agree, but for the sake of this article, I am dealing with love in a generic sense, and its development requires further explanation.

The thrust of this vision is that God is more than one person in an equal, loving, creative relationship. That truth is reflected not just in the personal make-up of man, but also in the structure of the local church. Leadership of the local congregations in the New Testament is described as elders, plural, and just as Father God is first amongst equals of the Trinity, so it is in the local congregation; there is headship in the eldership. During the Reformation, the Anglican Church recognized this difference and, to avoid the errors of papal domination, they declared the Archbishop of Canterbury to be "The First amongst Equals" amid the bishops by an Act of Parliament during the reign of King Henry VIII.

---

487   Luke 22:42 (NIV).
488   Luke 3:22b (NIV).
489   John 14:26 (TLB).

The interdependent relationship of love as expressed in the Trinity is the *model for all our relationships*. No other model will work. Our man-made attempts plunge us into power struggles of control and domination, whether it's husband and wife, family, business, government, or especially church. We work with imperfect people, but that doesn't change the reality that we have to become love just like our God. The application and development of this message is more than we can share in this brief article, but unless we have this *god pattern* as our foundation, what we build will be flawed in concept and application.

For our encouragement, God promises that if we submit to Him in everything, just as Jesus did, we will be able to love just like Jesus does. This has to be the greatest message of all time—man becoming like God and becoming *love*: "*And we know that all that happens to us is working for our good if we love God and are fitting into his plans.*"[490] The Apostle John writes:

> *Dear friends, let us practice loving each other, for love comes from God and those who are loving and kind show that they are the children of God, and they are getting to know him better. But if a person isn't loving and kind, it shows that he doesn't know God—for* **God is love***.*"[491] (emphasis added)

Shalom.

---

490 Romans 8:28 (TLB).
491 1 John 4:7–8 (TLB).

WORKS CITED

Centers for Disease Control and Prevention. "Sexually Transmitted Diseases." https://www.cdc.gov/msmhealth/STD.htm (accessed June 1, 2018).

Christensen, Jen. "LGBQ Teens Face Serious Suicide Risk, Research Finds." CNN.com. https://www.cnn.com/2017/12/19/health/lgbq-teens-suicide-risk-study/index.html

Cooke, Graham. *A Divine Confrontation.* (Shippensburg, PA: Destiny Image, 2000).

Edwards, Gene. *A Tale of Three Kings.* (Carol Stream, IL: Tyndale House Publishers, 1992).

Fong, Betty. "Damaging Effects of Too Much Sugar." Livestrong.com. https://www.livestrong.com/article/144711-damaging-effects-of-too-much-sugar-in-diet/ (accessed June 1, 2018).

Goldschmidt, Vivian. "New Report: More Deaths Caused by Prescription Drugs than by Car Accidents." Saveinstitute.com. https://saveourbones.com/more-deaths-caused-by-prescription-drugs-than-by-car-accidents/ (accessed June 1, 2018).

Joyner, Rick. *The Call.* (Charlotte, NC: Morningstar Publications, 2006).

Joyner, Rick. *World Aflame.* (Charlotte, NC: Morningstar Publications, 1993).

Keller, Timothy. *The Reason for God.* (New York: Penguin Group, Inc, 2008).

Lawrence, Br. and Laubach, Frank. *Practicing His Presence* (Goleta, CA: Christian Books, 1976).

Lewis, C.S. *Mere Christianity.* (San Francisco, CA: HarperCollins Publishers, 1952).

Lewis, C.S. *The Great Divide.* (New York: HarperCollins Publishers, 2001).

OECD. "Obesity Update 2017." https://politics.ucsc.edu/undergraduate/chicago%20style%20guide.pdf (accessed June 1, 2018).

Phillips, J.B. *Letters to Young Churches: A Translation of the New Testament Epistles.* (London: Geoffrey Bless, 1954).

Also by Ron Harris

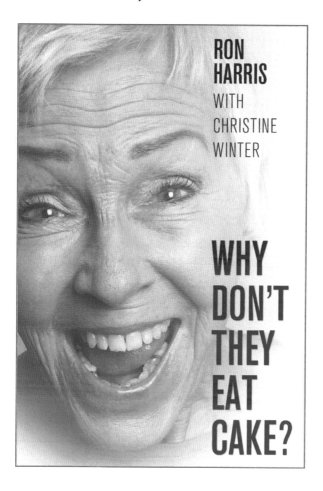

One of the greatest challenges in life is to have empathy and understanding for those outside of our culture, timeframe, and life experiences. Those of us who have children and grandchildren often become exasperated by their seeming blindness to the challenges we faced in our day. Some of the articles in this book make a lame attempt at bridging that gap. I have even attempted to look at life from God's point of view but with some risk of divine correction, so I am very thankful we have a merciful God. Why would I travel such a sensitive road? Well, in the climate of these articles … it is because I can! Our society falls into the trap of judging the past from the immediate present, but this does not explain the hopes and life experiences of an earlier generation. As in my first book, no subject is sacrosanct from a Christian world view. Enjoy the read!